GW00854409

How To Compete
Successfully
In Your Own Field

by Hubert Bermont

Published by
BERMONT BOOKS

twenty dollars

PREVIOUS BOOKS BY THE AUTHOR

Psychoanalysis Is A Great Big Help!, Stein & Day, 1963

Have You Read A Good Book Lately?, Stein & Day, 1964

Mine Son, The Samurai, Pocket Books, 1965

The Child, Pocket Books, 1965

The Mother, Simon & Schuster, 1968

All God's Children, Stein & Day, 1968

New Approaches To Financing Parks & Recreation,
Acropolis Books, 1970

Jonathan Livingston Fliegle, Dell, 1973

Getting Published, Fleet Press, 1973, Harper,
and Row, 1974

How To Become A Successful Consultant In Your Own Field,
Bermont Books, 1978

The Handbook Of Association Book Publishing, Bermont
Books, 1978

*The Successful Consultant's Guide to Authoring, Publishing
& Lecturing*, Bermont Books, 1979

ISBN 0-930686-05-5

BERMONT BOOKS
815 15th St., N.W.
Washington, D.C. 20005

Printed in the United States of America

Table Of Contents

Introduction

Contrary to public opinion, success is easier to achieve today in the United States than ever before. But fewer Americans than ever before consider themselves successful; and, indeed, they are not. Endowed with eight cylinders, we generally operate on one. Nor have we changed much (except for the worse) since Harry David Thoreau called us a "nation of sleepwalkers."

Since, in the country of the blind the one-eyed man is king, it follows that in a nation of sleepwalkers, semi-functional "professionals," one-cylinder businessmen and general under-achievers at large, the highly aware, motivated and functional person must enjoy the fruits of success.

You have every right to demand here and now, at the outset, that I define "success" as it applies

INTRODUCTION

to this book. Very well. But first, allow me to state what it is not. Success is not money alone, it is not the power to manipulate and control others, and it is not an arbitrary, artificial title. Success is peace of mind, it is the respect of self and the respect from others in your field, it is the bottom-line of the financial sheet which tells you that you may continue in your chosen line of work without fear or worry, and it is the ability to look into the mirror and see a true *professional*.

I find it both interesting and indicative that I started with the words "contrary to public opinion." I hope, trust and expect that you will find this entire book contrary to public opinion. For it is public opinion, deliberately and satanically shaped by our "leaders," which has led us astray and taken our collective eye off the true goal of life - - - individual success. Hopefully, too, this book will help you to focus more clearly on your singular goal and then show you the simple - - - but not easy - - - ways to achieve it.

I. The Death Of The Salesman

I. The Death Of The Salesman

The cliché is a much maligned, hence underused
phrase in our literature and textbooks today. This
is most unfortunate, since, when applicable, we can
find no better aphoristic truth. So, without apo-
logy, I shall use them freely.

There is very little room at the top in your
field and mine. But not everyone can be a Chief;
many must be Indians. Indeed, were we all Chiefs,
no one would be recognized as one. However, follow-
ers don't buy and read "how-to" books like this.
You obviously want to rise up in your line of work
and leave the crowd behind.

The road up from the bottom is the *selling*
road. It's such a pity that the word "sales" has
been used so pejoratively in our society over the
past two generations. "He's a born salesman" used

to be a high accolade. Today it means that he or
she is a conniver, a liar, a con-man, or someone
who will soon separate you from your money against
your will. So we shun the title and even the activity of the salesman. And that's how we got off
the road and lost our way.

Along with this, we have allowed the meaning
of "competitive" to get twisted out of shape. Society today avoids anyone who is called "competitive."
It is assumed that this person is out to slaughter
you on his or her way up. There is no truth to
this, of course, as we shall learn later, but this
is the commonly accepted fallacy.

In all pyramidal societies, everyone starts at
the base or bottom. Here the word definitions - - -
which always shape our values - - - have never changed.
No one wants to be at the bottom. Adjectivally, "base"
means inferior. To rise from this lowly position requires competitiveness manifested by exhibiting one or
more outstanding qualities not apparent in the rest of
the herd. And this exhibitionism or attention-getting
is the first sign of *advertising,* another filthy word
today. We must start by advertising and selling ourselves. And we can never quit - - - ever. Strip
away the negative connotations of the words, which
were applied by the base, lazy people in our society
in the first place. You couldn't possibly feel, as
they do, that life can be fulfilled by standing still
and never bettering yourself.

Sure, on one level, the rags-to-riches story
of Horatio Alger, is laughable. Aside from being
poor literature, it is an exaggeration and a dis-
tortion of the real world. But take more credible
examples. Take Bernard Baruch, or even his steno-
grapher, Billy Rose. Too famous and out-of-reach?
Then take a clerk in a department store, who is at
the base of that particular retailing pyramid. After
several days of training and trying to learn the
nature and applicability of the many and various
forms to be filled out, he or she will be confused.
Months later, after experience and use, these forms
will be handled efficiently and expeditiously. What
about the clerk, who, on his own, decided to write
a manual, explaining in detail for future new clerks
how and when to fill out a charge slip, a C.O.D. slip,
an extended payment transaction, a credit slip, a refund, etc.? What about this being the attention-
getter? What about a reward in the form of a ten-
dollar-a-week raise? Isn't this *selling* in the true
sense? Isn't this advertising? Isn't this competitive? Did this hurt anyone else? Isn't this the
first step on the road to success?

O.K., you may say, but what if it goes unnoticed by management. Well, what if it does? A
fertile mind like that, motivated by a striving
to get ahead, will do a number of such things in
the course of a year. If still unnoticed by that
time, the clerk can take advantage of the marvelous
freedom in this country by quitting and going else-

where - - - someplace where he or she will be appre-
ciated. But never, never should he squelch the
competitive, advertising, selling spirit. "What's
the use? They don't appreciate me. The world is
unfair," is a cop-out. Over the long haul, the
private sector of the world is eminently fair - - -
and that's what the ne'er-do-wells detest. It is
the public sector which is unfair; it attempts to
invert the natural pyramid by rewarding those at the
base and stifling and villifying those who have
reached or are about to reach the top. Any attempt
to tamper with the bureaucratic pyramid, however, is
scotched in short order.

Let's go back even further before one enters
the working world. When I was a senior in college,
we were occasionally visited by a successful alumnus
who lectured us on getting ahead in the real world out
there after graduation. One such visitor, the president of a large corporation, told this story from
behind his lectern:

> I recently had to promote some young executive
> in our firm to the position of assistant to the
> president (myself). After much screening and
> selection by our personnel division, the choice
> came down to two bright people, whom I shall call
> Mr. Brown and Mr. Green. I interviewed each of
> them myself and for the life of me could not
> choose between them. Each was of equal intelli-
> gence and ability, and each had the same perfect
> record with the company. I decided to reserve
> my decision for awhile. Several weeks later, I
> was the main speaker at a corporation dinner. As
> I sat at the head table, waiting to be introduced
> and making last-minute notes, I found myself out

of cigarettes. I asked the waiter to bring
some, but he explained that he couldn't leave
the dining room. I became fidgety and obviously
nervous, being addicted to nicotine. Out of
nowhere, Mr. Brown appeared behind me and quietly and unobtrusively placed a pack of my particular brand of cigarettes alongside my plate.
Without a word, he then withdrew. That one act
made my decision in favor of Mr. Brown.

The next day, the headline of our college daily newspaper screamed "ALUMNUS PREACHES APPLE-POLISHING AS
GUARANTEE FOR SUCCESS." (I suppose that today's
headline would have substituted a stronger synony-
mous phrase for "apple-polishing.") The reporter
then went on to damn the alumnus, his philosophy,
the college (for allowing him to speak), and the
corporate world in general. The campus was in an
uproar. If that's the way the business community
was out there, we wanted no part of it. But we
were young and foolish - - - as young and foolish
as are older people who still think this way. We,
like others, couldn't accept the reality of the
world, and so refused to look at it. On another
level, we were already creating excuses for our
own possible future failures.

Today the man's story makes all kinds of
sense. He was telling us to think at all times,
to be inventive even on the most mundane levels,
to keep striving to do just a little bit better
and a little bit more than the next person alongside us, to keep placing little advertisements for

ourselves and to keep selling at all times. In
short, he was "telling it like it was" in the business arena. It still is that way, even though society scoffs at it and refuses to recognize it. The
results have been as ludicrous and dire as those
derived from our not "recognizing" the 900,000,000
people of China for so many years.

And it's not just a question of selling once
to rise from the bottom of the pyramid. It's a
question of selling *always* to rise to the top. Then
it's a question of *continuing* to sell in order to *stay*
there. That is where even the most successful companies, professionals, and even our country fall
apart.

Why has the United States slipped so far down
in the world order of economics? Because of the
dollar? Because of the oil crises? Because of the
international political upheavals? Not at all. It
is because we have refused to compete in the world
marketplace; because we have set up protective
tarrifs; because we are frightened of competition.
It is because most of the salesmen have quietly
passed away here, and no one has mourned their
deaths.

When I was a boy, there were much fewer auto-
mobiles manufactured than there are today. The
competition wasn't nearly as keen. Yet, at least
once a month, my father would get a phone call from

an automobile salesman at a local showroom, inviting
him to see a new model car. If my father demurred,
the salesman would offer to bring the car to our
house to be test-driven. I recall that he bought
a new 1934 Chevrolet sedan for $735 as a result of
that sales approach. Have you or I received a call
like that in the last thirty years? Do you feel
sorry for a dealer or salesman who sits on his duff
and waits for us to come in and buy a $9,000 car (as
a result of his silly advertising), all the while
complaining that his sales are off 18%? When you
walk into the average retail store, don't you get
the feeling that you are bothering and intruding upon the average salesclerk? When was the last time
the clerk used suggestive selling so that you left
the store with two purchases instead of one? When
was the last time you were even thanked for the
transaction?

Speaking of merchandising and suggestive selling, remember the story of the woman who went into
the furniture/hardware store in a New England town?
The owner drove his sales staff tirelessly, unmerci-
fully and endlessly. He would sit behind his roll-
top desk on the balcony and watch his trade like a
hawk. He saw this particular customer ask for something, saw the salesman shake his head, and watched
furiously as the lady left his store empty-handed.
He came flying down the stairs, demanding to know
why the sale was lost. "She wanted a blanket,"
said the salesman, "and we don't carry them." "So

what, you muttonhead," screamed the proprietor,
"we have Franklin stoves, don't we?" Don't you
miss merchants like that who really want your business? Or do you prefer the ones we have who tell
you that you can't bring food or drink into their
stores, that they won't give you change for the
parking meter, that they won't cash your check,
that you need at least two pieces of identification
before they will accept your check as payment, that
if you knock something over you'll have to pay for
it, that they accept no merchandise for refund unless they take your photograph, that you are being
watched by closed-circuit security television cam-
eras, that parking is not free unless you buy something, and so on *ad nauseum.* Isn't it nice to buy
something from someone who appreciates your business?

The bigger they are, the harder they fall.
Robert Hall, W.T. Grant, *et al.* This trouble comes
from the attitude "We've made it. We don't have
to try anymore." Well, you might say, it's a
terrible prospect to keep striving forever without
being able to let up; life must hold more promise
than that. No! That's what life is all about!
It is this very strife that keeps us alive. Ask
anyone who has quit. Ask any retiree with talent.
(More about this in the final chapter.)

But most important, it's the constant peak
of performance that will keep you at the top. I

once bought a Yamaha piano. Other piano manufacturers look enviously upon Yamaha, their high quality standards and their low prices, and say, "They've
got it made." But wait; the Yamaha people don't
think they've "got it made." One month after my
purchase, I received an air-mail letter from Japan
reminding me of both my guarantee and free tuning
and requesting that I take full advantage of them
for the protection of my instrument. A month after
that came another letter from Japan. This one required that I let them know whether or not my local
dealer was adhering to all of their customer policies and whether or not he was doing so politely.
During the third month I received an air-mailed
package. It was wrapped as only the Japanese can
exquisitely wrap a gift. Inside was a hand-made
doll of infinite beauty. A short accompanying note
thanked me for my purchase and for selecting a
Yamaha. Can we compete with this? Shouldn't we?
How can they help but be successful? How many more
pianos do you think they have sold as a result of my
recommendation? Can Madison Avenue meet this kind of
advertising competition? Especially on such a low
budget?

The kind of selling we are discussing here
requires *human effort*. Throwing money at it won't
help. But the musculature we once had for this
kind of human effort seems to have atrophied. Instead, when a modern American man is called a crack-
erjack salesman, he usually gets angry and says,

THE DEATH OF THE SALESMAN

"Don't call me that. I'm a marketing specialist."
The day is soon coming when a sales conference will
be raided by the authorities more quickly than a
massage parlor.

All we hear today is "I want to get out of
sales and get into something *creative*." Really!
And where would all of those "creative" people be
today if someone weren't out there creatively selling what they have produced? Collecting unemployment compensation, that's where. If society insists
upon maligning the sales effort, we can do nothing
about it. But if you and I individually reflect
that attitude by disparaging our own efforts to sell
ourselves, our wares, our services and our companies,
then we are doomed to failure. If we cannot tune
them out, then we cannot turn ourselves on.

II. The Creative Art Of Selling

II. The Creative Art Of Selling

Another way of expressing a major principle of the previous chapter is this: If a salesman regards his encounters with customers as pitched battles, if he indeed feels that he is the perpetrator of a con-game, and if he feels that at the end of each trans-action one "contestant" wins and the other one loses, he is doomed to a life of utter frustration and ul-timate failure. This was explained to me when I was a very young salesman in a retail store by a top-notch man who always went home with the biggest commission check. At that time, he had over thirty years of experience. Having armed myself with as much information about our wares as possible (I prided myself on the fact that I had as much tech-nical information as the old-timer), I went into combat with all customers: wheedling, cajoling, charming, telling jokes and even threatening them with the consequences of their not buying. I did

this with what I thought were the battle-lines
clearly drawn, i.e. I was the "good guy" trying
and needing to make sales to support my new young
family, and they were the "bad guys" trying to
prevent me from making those sales. After each
sale - - - which occurred infrequently - - - I was
emotionally exhausted. Mr. Experience had no such
days. He was easygoing, calm and lost very few
sales. One day, he took me aside and said, "Kid,
I like you. That's why I'm going to explain to
you why you have the wrong approach and the wrong
attitude. These customers aren't your enemies.
Nor do they wander into this store by accident or
to come in out of the rain. They come here for a
reason: *to make a purchase.* You come on either as
though they're in here to give you a rough time,
as though it's your duty to remind them that they
came in to buy something and as though nothing
could be further from their minds. They have a
genuine need for what we exhibit and sell, but they
are confused and frightened. These are tough times
economically and they work hard for their money.
They are terribly concerned about making a financial mistake by buying something expensive that
they neither need nor want. But they do need and/
or want something, or they wouldn't be here. Your
job is to calm them and *help* them part with the money
they actually do want to spend; your job is not to
fight them and try to grab their money away from
them because of your own needs. Their needs come
first. We salesmen are so fortunate in that the

satisfying of our customers' material desires happens to *coincide* with our needs. Now, once you have made the sale, you aren't finished. You must continue the selling process to dispel any residual doubts in their minds when they get home. You must be certain that they leave this store feeling that they have made an *acquisition* rather than a *purchase*."

At another point in my selling career (substitute the word "education"), I was a sales representative for a high-quality no-name brand manufacturer. Twice every year, the president of the company held a sales conference to introduce us to his new line of products. He would go over every detail of each item carefully, show us how well it was made and explain the price structure. At one such meeting, one of the salesmen complained, "How can you expect us to sell this line to our trade in the face of the huge advertising budgets of the name brands? You never advertise at all. Nobody has ever heard of this company. The name-brand companies' reps just breeze in and out of our customers' stores with fat orders, while we must struggle for every small sale we get. Why not face it? They've got the market knocked up." The president looked at him quizzically and then simply said, "Turn in your sample-bag and order forms. You're fired." We were all shocked. That salesman had been with the firm for eight years and had done a pretty good job. After the man left the room, I asked why such sudden and abrupt action was taken. The president answered me by addressing us all. He said, "My father before me started this company fifty years ago. He had a valid reason for going into business. He felt strongly that he could build a better product for less money than the name-brand companies, which were sitting at the top of the heap at that time, too. He did build a better product for less money, and a small, but important segment of the market bought it. He was right. My brothers and I followed in his footsteps by continuing the same policies. Of course it's more difficult to sell 'Brand X'. I know that. It is for this reason that you men get twice the percentage of commission as those guys who 'breeze in and out' of your customers' stores with fat orders. They don't have to sell very hard. You do. But the only way you *can* sell my line is by believing that it is twice the value for half the price - - - by believing the truth, because it is. I take all that advertising money and put it into the production process. That salesman no longer believed in my products, so I fired him. I did us both a favor. When you stop believing in your product, you can't sell it anymore. Put another way, when you believe that your competitor's product is as good as or better than yours, you can't sell. I never ask any of my men to go out there and pull the wool over anyone's eyes. I know that I make a fine product at a very competitive price, and I ask that you sell it. If you don't believe in my line and if you don't think it will sell, I don't want you representing my company."

Simple as that. You must *believe* to sell. Not
by a leap of faith, but by honest comparison with
your competition. Rip-offs play such hell with
your conscience that you will lose your self-
respect - - - and self-respect is the prime requisite for success in the business and professional
worlds.

I learned two more lessons about the creative
art of selling. One, again by a top pro, and the
other on my own by accident. At this stage of my
career (education) I had my own establishment.

I was losing sales I couldn't afford to lose.
I seemed to reach excellent rapport with prospective customers and they, in turn, seemed to trust
and like me, my merchandise and my prices. But
there was a final moment of indecision that I
couldn't overcome. "I have to talk it over with
my wife (husband)." "Let me go home and think
about it." "I'll definitely call you tomorrow."
I just couldn't close those sales. I set up a
meeting with a salesman who was earning $75,000
a year in commissions. I explained my plight. He
said something I never forgot. "As long as you are
going to strike out anyhow, why don't you strike
out swinging?" I thought I *was* swinging. He
explained, "Why don't you simply ask the *customers*
why you are not closing the sale? Since they like
you, since they like the merchandise and since they

like the prices, why are they hesitating? Instead
of asking *me* why they are walking out without buying, why don't you ask *them?* In other words, I
think you are forgetting the most crucial, final
step. You are forgetting to ask for the sale!"
Well, I tried that. I asked the very next customer
who faltered why he was hesitating. He looked puz-
zled and then said, "I really don't know why; I have
no reason. Write it up. I'll buy it now." This
simple question closed eight out of ten such prospective sales. By simply swinging, I didn't strike
out half as often.

I had never been aware of how much my tensions
and anxieties about selling communicated themselves
to my customers, until the day after my son was born.
This was an event in my life which completely over-
shadowed my business, my sales and my profits. I
just wasn't thinking about success that day - - -
only about being a new father. As each customer
approached me and intruded upon my parental thoughts,
I honestly apologized by saying, "Forgive me for
not paying complete attention to business today.
You see, we had a baby yesterday." Every customer
empathized by asking whether it was a boy or a girl,
how much the baby weighed, whether this was my first
(accompanied by much advice), how mother and child
were doing and how I was holding up emotionally.
As though it was incidental, every customer made
a major purchase without any salestalk from me at
all. The cameraderie continued this way for two

days, and I made a bundle of money. (To prove that this could only work if genuine, I tried to use "We had a baby yesterday," as a selling line three months later; nobody bought it.) What I learned was the efficacy of being relaxed while selling. Lao Tze, the ancient Chinese philosopher, called it the usefulness of uselessness. Your desperate need for the commission or profit from a sale isn't and shouldn't be the customer's business. If revealed, it puts him off. He knows then that you do not have his best interests at heart.

I have carried these five lessons with me always in every field of endeavor:

1. If you sell well, you are doing your customer a favor.

2. The primary concern must be for the customer's welfare, not your own.

3. If you are going to strike out, strike out swinging.

4. You must believe in what you are selling or doing.

5. Relax. You are engaged in something worthwhile, not in a war.

III. Incentive

III. Incentive

The best definition I know for "incentive" is *caring*. No one can compete, strive, sell or succeed if he doesn't care. This means caring deeply about your business, caring about your reputation and ultimately caring about yourself. This brings us to another piece of hard-nosed reality which most of us refuse to accept: *nobody will ever care as much for your business as you do*. An employee, no matter how high in your table of organization and no matter how well compensated cannot care about your company as much as you do. Also, a computer can think for you, but it can never care. More businesses fall apart by being entrusted to other people and machines than for any other reason. The common (and appropriate) attitude of both employees and computers is that problems are figuratively and literally none of their business.

INCENTIVE

A man I know built a successful company from the ground up. After thirty-five years, he reached a point where he felt that he wanted to work only six months a year. He was now sixty-four years old. So he hired a bright young man, taught him the business, paid him well and gave him the reins. At a particular trade convention, the two men brought their wives for three days to combine business with pleasure. At the end of that month, my friend observed that his own convention expenses totaled $350, whereas the young executive vice-president and his wife cost the corporation $1100. My friend was extremely upset and hurt. "I gave him everything. I treated him like a son. And now he does this to me and my company." He fired the man forthwith. Of course, the young executive was stupid; he ruined a good thing for himself, because he was a very short distance from the presidency. But my friend wasn't too smart, either, in that he refused to see the reality of this all-too-common situation. That reality was perfectly expressed in his own tale of woe. "And now he does this to me and my company." Exactly: *his* company, not the other guy's. And only the owner can care that much about his own company.

Some time ago, I saw a wonderful cartoon in a magazine. It shows a well-to-do-looking business-man just arriving home at the end of the day. He is standing in his elegant foyer and his dutiful wife is taking his hat and coat. He says to her, "I've done it, Mildred. I fired them all - - - all

3286 of them. I'll go it alone." Every businessman I know can identify with that absurd line.

Norman Rockwell's paintings and characters
are all fictive. Even he knew that. They aren't
nostalgic, because our country and our people simply never were that way. We seem to have this
terrible habit of trying to wish dreams into reality and then dreaming that we have succeeded. The
totally loyal employee who cares as much or more
about his employer's business is a fiction, as well
it should be. He doesn't have as much incentive as
his employer. He may put out extra, uncalled-for
effort for fear of losing his job; but he will not
have the interest that the owner has, since he has
no financial investment.

Here is an example. During the past ten
years, I have been hearing the same inanity over
and over from salespeople and it drives me up a
wall. If they are temporarily out of a popular
item - - - which should never happen in the first
place - - - they invariably say, "It sells so fast,
we can't keep it in stock." This is just another
way of saying that there is no one "minding" the
store. Of course, this always occurs in a chain
operation, where the principal has lost control.
No respectable shopkeeper in his right mind would
admit publicly that he doesn't know unit control
or stock reordering principles well enough to keep
a fast-moving item flowing regularly into and out

of his store. In other words, I never heard this
kind of idiocy from an owner, only from an employee.
An owner never throws up his hands in despair; he
always finds ways to do business.

What to do in a society where the average
employee has lost sight of the fact that his or her
salary is dependent upon company earnings? What to
do in a society where the government can slap an
injunction against a corporation in the throes of
bankruptcy due to heavy financial loss, on the
grounds that the bankruptcy would create too much
unemployment? What to do when there *is* work that
you must delegate to others in order to give you
time to make your company grow? We really can't
"go it alone," but we can't succeed by employing
"warm bodies" either.

There are two ways to combat these syndromes
so that you may move ahead. One way is to use as
many outside services as possible; those people
have the same incentive as you do to make their
individual enterprises grow. A second way is to
hire at the lowest legal minimum wage with a high
incentive commission based on individual work output, not on the earnings of the corporation.

None of the other intricate "incentive" plans
seem to work. Giving employees shares of stock in
the corporation, offering liberal end-of-year
bonuses if the company does well or giving extreme-

ly liberal fringe benefits and executive per-
quisites have produced nothing in the way of increased incentive or performance. Again, these
plans are based upon what we think people should
be, but not on what we are. They are formulated
by brilliant folks who don't understand that nine-
ty percent of the human race is incapable of ab-
straction. The average person can only deal with
the here and now. Not only is the concept of a
share of corporate stock too complicated, but fringe
benefits and "perks" are quickly regarded as salary.
And to be fair about it, why should an employee have
his earnings tied to that of the corporation when he
is not in any way connected with the decision-making
process? Nor am I recommending that we embrace the
new foolish movement afoot which is demanding that
labor shape policy equally with management; that
way leads to sheer chaos. Firstly, labor has no
financial investment and could never care as much
as management; secondly, an elephant is a greyhound
which has been redesigned by a committee.

Since most people can neither abstract nor
postpone, the immediate reward can be the only
incentive. Piece-work, high sales commissions
and instant time off when a particular job is completed; these are the things that everyone can understand, appreciate and be motivated by. But to
accomplish this, every job must be clearly defined
and described. Too often today, the average employee doesn't seem to have a clear grasp of what

35

he is expected to do, nor is he sufficiently
trained to do it well. Less and less time is
spent in training. More and more time is spent
dealing with high personnel turnover (not to mention the cost). The result is generally a bunch
of disinterested people hanging around, waiting to
quit or be replaced. The employer who claims he
doesn't have the time to diligently train his employees reminds me of the mother who doesn't have
the twenty minutes it would take to train her five-
year-old to tie his own shoes - - - she spends 260
hours for the next few years tying his shoes for
him.

I mentioned piece-work awhile back, and I
don't want to skip over it lightly, because it always raises all kinds of eyebrows. The term "piece-
work" conjures up the old sweatshops of yesteryear
where men, women and children worked in intolerable
conditions fourteen to twenty hours a day, and were
woefully underpaid. That was a different time in a
different economy. It goes without saying that
neither child labor nor hazardous working conditions
should be tolerated; and the minimum wage (which is
not a living wage) can be set as the floor. But
above that, there should be a goodly price paid for
the labor of everything produced, whether goods or
services. This restores incentive to the point
where quality is once again put into the end product; concomitantly, pride is restored to the work-
force. Here is an example. When a salaried shipping

clerk sees a huge new load of merchandise arrive
on his work-table, he always moans and groans - - -
naturally, it's just that much more work for him to
do. But if he were to get, let us say, fifty
cents for each package shipped, he would virtually
pray as hard as his employer does for more business.
It never fails. One thousand more parcels to ship
out puts five hundred more dollars into his pocket
immediately. No amount of shares of stock, no retirement plan and no iffy end-of-the year bonus can
match this.

But we continue to treat people as though they
are something other than people.

IV. The Goal Of Excellence

IV. The Goal Of Excellence

Perfection is something that none of us can ever attain, but it is something we should all constantly strive to achieve. This said, we must define "perfection" before making it our goal.

Excellence, or perfection in business is the following:

1. The ability to look ahead with confidence in the fact that your business will not go under.

2. The ability to extract the most financial profit from what you are doing.

3. A continuous modicum of company growth in profit, share of market and reputation to accommodate our inflationary economy.

4. The cutting back on expenses wherever possible so that basic overhead never gets so high that it cannot be met during

an occasional slump.

But to accomplish all of this requires excellence and perfection in ourselves, since we must
at all times be at the helms of our own ships.
How to do this in the business world?

The first goal is information. We cannot
lead or act wisely if we are uninformed. Information
is available concentrically (in circles). Too few
businessmen take the time to read their own trade
periodicals cover-to-cover. There you generally
find out what's happening in your trade or profession, what your competition is doing, the cur-
rent state of the art, and prognostications about
the future. The next outward concentric circle of
information is contained in professional and textbooks relating to your particular field.

A word here about rapid reading for those of
you who constantly complain that you have no time
for books. Accurate, information-gathering, com-
prehensive reading ability cannot be acquired by
means of the popular "rapid reading" courses offered to the public. They merely increase your
stop-watch speed in direct proportion to your loss
of attention-span and comprehension. The element
of personal curiosity is the primary requisite for
real rapid reading. You are reading for information.
This means that you must have mental unanswered questions beforehand. Approach the book and its author

with these questions in mind. Address yourself
first to the table of contents and/or the index
to determine whether or not this writer is dealing
at all with the things you personally want to know.
If not, discard this book; you are not reading for
entertainment or for a general education. If the
book does deal with your areas in question, go
immediately to those sections and try to extract
the answers; sometimes you will find them, and
sometimes not. The second rule of rapid reading
is to skip over that which doesn't interest you.
Just because something is in print doesn't mean
that it is holy scripture and must be read. The
third rule is to ignore any writer whose style is
such that you cannot be his communicant. There
are as many writers like that as there are people
you ignore who are inarticulate.

Move now to the next outer layer of information - - - your local newspaper. Not just the
financial pages. Every section every day has
something which directly or indirectly affects
your business - - - including the advertisements.
Your newspaper may not give you a totally realistic
picture of what the world is like (you must rely
upon your own intellect for that), but it does give
you an accurate picture of how your community is
perceiving that world and, therefore, how its
attitudes and values are being shaped and formed.
You need this knowledge desperately for your own
success in your business.

THE GOAL OF EXCELLENCE

Moving further outward, we come to national magazines and newspapers like *The New York Times* and *The Wall Street Journal*. These give us both in-depth information and a wider perspective. If your business is to grow, you cannot afford to be either xenophobic or provincial in your outlook. And then, finally, in my own case, I read *The International Herald Tribune* for a global view of what's going on.

The second goal of excellence is to become as much of a central switchboard as possible, with the plugs connected to its ultimate capacity. By this I mean make as many business contacts as you possibly can in every direction: colleagues, peers, resources, suppliers, trade or professional association people, and customers and clients. This is the human source of experiential knowledge; cold print is not enough. The thoughts, concepts and reactions of other people in your field are invaluable nuggets for your information mill. Phone calls, lunches, quick notes, articles via mail, requests for reaction to events are all welcome by those people out there. Every time I embark on a major project, I carefully go through my wheeldex file to see who out there might inform or help me. Ofttimes, good friendships develop, and the free, honest exchange of information between real friends in the same field cannot be duplicated; whatever knowledge you bring to such a relationship becomes automatically doubled. Those who are mistrusting of others and who always feel that everyone else in the field is their cut-throat competitor will automatically miss out on a vital exchange of information. The vacuum that these people create for themselves is stifling and counter-productive.

Ultimately, excellence implies becoming the very best in your industry or profession. It is important, of course, that you are recognized as such by your peers. But it is even more important that *you* know yourself to be the best. You will recognize this when you have become single-minded in your purpose and have cleared your life of extraneous matters.

V. The Laser Mind

V. The Laser Mind

J. Paul Getty once wrote a book on how to become
a millionaire. Without judging Getty one way or
another, it can be safely said that he had one
very important thing going for him: he understood
and accepted his own priorities and goals very
early in life and *single-mindedly* set out to achieve
them. In his case, he simply wanted to amass an
enormous amount of money - - - and he did. He
allowed absolutely nothing to deter or deflect
him from his course. Even when he bemoaned the
fact that he didn't take the time to gaze upon
and enjoy his art collection in various parts of
the world, he knew that he simply didn't think it
important enough to interfere with his life's work
- - - making money.

It matters not whether you or I agree that
making millions for their own sake is a fit and

proper ambition and lifetime occupation. Someone
else may look askance at or belittle *our* careers.
What is essential is that we are single-minded in
our purpose and that we give it everything we've
got.

Nor is it a question of becoming or not becoming a "well-rounded person" - - - whatever that
is supposed to mean. I never heard anyone describe
himself or herself as not being well-rounded. I
have heard people describe *others* that way. If you
are an outer-directed person, you will allow what
others think of you to interfere with your purpose. If
you are an inner-directed person, nothing can get
in your way. Since it is endemic to the nature of
a politican to care deeply about what others (voters)
think of him, he never accomplishes anything.

There is one sure-fire way to become an inner-
directed person. With regard to your attitude towards your own activities, simply remove the concepts of "I should," "I shouldn't," I ought" and
"I ought not" from your mental vocabulary. They
are invariably geared to a need for societal appro-
bation; and society doesn't have the foggiest idea
about anything at all.

Establishing your own priorities is not difficult. You know what your life's work is. You know
how far and how high you want to go with it. And,
when you honestly get right down to it, you really

know what you have to do to get there. If you don't have sufficient dedication to make the commitment, then you are lying to yourself and you really don't have goals - - - you have fantasies. Goals can be actualized, fantasies cannot.

In my own case, I recently founded a small publishing company. Everything started to come together for me very quickly and success (on my own terms) seemed imminent. I became totally immersed and involved in my new enterprise. For the first time in my life, I found myself working ten and twelve hours a day, six and seven days a week. But what amazed me most was that I found myself *enjoying* this regimen. I had been an amateur tennis-player for thirty years, but gave it up. I had been a musician of sorts all of my life, but no longer went near my piano. One day, I found myself clucking along with my friends and family who felt that my giving up these leisure activities was a shame. But then I realized that I had done it willfully and voluntarily. I had merely re-set my priorities. I became so fascinated with my new enterprise that it seemed totally unimportant to me anymore whether or not a tennis ball I hit went over the net or who won the set. I was winning at something far more spectacular for me. My work had become my leisure. *My vocation had become my avocation!*

The mind must indeed be laser-like for the work to succeed. Why isn't the mind this way in

most cases? What are the forces "out there" which
prohibit us from operating on all eight cylinders,
which deflect us from true achievement, and which
make us fade out while rounding third base en route
to home plate?

Well, in the first place, two eminent psychiatrists have proven that we shall never identify or
locate those forces if we continue looking for them
"out there." They are within us - - - each of us.
Sigmund Freud said, in effect "Be careful what you
wish for; you might get it." Karl Menninger said
it in the title of his famous book *Man Against Himself*.
Work done well is one of the most satisfying things
given to man; visit any monastery and ask any monk,
and admire whatever it is they produce. Moreover,
success in work is a primary requisite to mastering
the art of living. Since most people fail and so
few succeed, Freud discovered that failure is much
more easily accepted than success. In point of
fact, psychiatrists' offices are filled with people
who have achieved success in their respective fields
and can't handle it emotionally. Failures usually
accept their plight easily. (This is the reason
that the affluent seek psychological help; not because they have the money to pay the fees. They
are in much more pain.)

The fact is, according to Menninger, we expend
far more psychic, mental and physical energy in trying to trip ourselves up on this road of life than

in paving our way. Although the theory is fascinating, it is something we should all fight with everything at our command.

What are some of the ways in which we diffuse our own lasers? Here are a few personal experiences by way of example.

Someone once gave me "an inside tip" on the stock market. Of course, you and I, in our saner moments, know that there is no such thing as "an inside tip" to an outsider. The only people who know what goes on in the stock market are those who are actually manipulating it for their own purposes. Well, it was one of my fuzzier days on which I was thinking like most of the other fuzzy-minded, i.e. not at all. I "reasoned" thus: If I can make a quick killing, I'll have that much more money (security) which, in turn, will give me more peace of mind so that I can work more calmly and relaxed in my own field. Simple? I should have remembered that the only person who ever made a killing at the market was the man who shot the manager of the A&P.

Well, I had $15,000 in savings at the time. I withdrew $10,000 of it and bought 1,000 shares of stock in a company I knew something about. Never was I so nervous in my entire life. I was awake at 5AM every day to grab the newspaper and see how my stock was doing. I wasn't even grateful that the market was closed on week-ends, because I objected

to the fact that my stock couldn't rise on Saturdays
and Sundays. I found myself dropping into brokerage
houses to watch the latest prices on their lit up
tote-boards. After awhile, I couldn't concentrate
on what I was doing in my office. Should I sell?
Should I buy more? Could I be wiped out? Could I
really afford to finance the next project in my
own business? Could I afford a vacation? Was I
rich? Was I poor? One thing was certain: I was
a wreck. I sold the stock, and went back to my
own work calmly and peacefully. I read the financial pages once again with the same objectivity as
I read any other news.

I had an accountant once who tried to persuade
me to buy some small housing as an investment. He,
too, said that I would make a killing. He was right
- - - in two ways. I would have made a lot of money,
real estate having soared the way it did; in another
sense, the killing would have been emotional sui-
cide, which, in turn, would have hurt my own career.
The thought of being a landlord with all that it
portends boggled my mind at the start. Amortization,
taxes, rents, regulations, complaints, etc. would
have all served to distract me and hurt my own business, which is not real estate.

Indeed, whatever success I have, I owe par-
tially to the fact that I have neither diluted nor
adulterated my work by doing any of those things.

I am certain that, conversely, the professional stock investor and real estate person would hinder their own careers by attempting to dip into anything that I do just to try for a fast buck.

The laser principle is the key.

VI. Anxiety Is The Mother Of Invention

VI. Anxiety Is The Mother Of Invention

We were reared and educated by a cruel and crip-
pling falsehood: since ours is a government "of the
people, by the people and for the people," the
government knows what's good for us. First, ours
is a government *by* influence peddlers. Second, ours
is a government *for* lobbyists and pressure groups.
Third, ours is a government of desensitized, alie-
nated, powerless taxpayers. And fourth, the government - - - whoever or whatever that is - - - hasn't
the foggiest idea of what's good for us, and cares
less. Our government is concerned only with feeding itself by governing more. It has been wisely
said that that government governs best which governs
least. Lao-Tse went one better by saying that that
government governs best which governs not at all.

The government, in its infinite dementia, has
created a welfare state. This has stripped most
citizens of two of the very valuable characteristics

59

(previously discussed) necessary for success: incentive and competitiveness. Why should the average citizen work when he can collect unemployment insurance and take home pretty much the same income? As the hen said to the farmer when she was reminded by him that her neighbor in the next roost was laying eggs which brought 25¢ more per dozen, "Why should I rip my ass for a quarter?" And why should we other "chickens" work as hard as we do to support those who don't? So we have a laid-back society. To me, a laid-back person is the same as a laid-out person. He might as well be dead.

But government has not yet won the day over human nature. It hasn't reckoned with anxiety and tension. Anxiety generally conjures up terrible things in our minds: neuroses, pain, physical ailments, etc. However, anxiety also produces creativity, a quest for self-respect, an impulse to prove something, and a need to produce something - - - anything. Anxiety has many causes, but one of the most common is *boredom*. By homogenizing us, stripping away our incentive, manipulating us, alienating us and attempting to reduce us to the most common denominator, government has made us bored to the eyeballs. Enter anxiety and tension - - - the kind that all of our sophisticated leisure activities combined are unable to quell.

We now have a life-and-death choice. Succumb to society or fight for our own individuality and

humanity. Consider the animals in zoos. They have
no choice. No matter how far zoologists go (and
how much money they spend) to create "natural sur-
roundings," the various species are never healthy
and become increasingly endangered. This is because they have lost their acumen and cunning for
the hunt. Since zoo-keepers cannot allow the
animals to naturally prey upon each other (they
would lose their zoos, hence their jobs), all
muscle-tone, agility, quickness of response and
reaction, alertness and prowess are lost. It is
left only for the animal to languish while waiting
for his next meal to be served. So, too, our keep-
ers (government) are trying to do the same number
on us. But we human animals have our anxieties to
help fight them.

Whenever the government lowers a standard, we
must raise it. Whenever a civil service employee
forgets that he or she is in "service," we must
scream like stuck pigs. (It came to my attention
recently that a small staff at the ICC rotated the
attendance at one of the desks in mid-afternoon so
that they could keep up with the soap-operas on
a TV set in a back office.) Whenever they want to
regulate more, we must howl. A friend of mine has
a large poster hanging in his office. It says:

"No man's life, liberty or property is safe
while the legislature is in session."

ANXIETY CREATES INVENTION

Armed with our tension and anxieties, we can allow our ingenuity, our incentive and our competitiveness full rein.

VII. Perseverance

VII. Perseverance

Remember the other awful lie we were taught?
"Everything comes to him who waits." Nonsense.
They were trying to teach us perseverance, and
what they should have said was "everything comes
to him who *works* - - - innovatively and with cunning." Here is another word which has fallen into
disrepute: cunning. We use it in admiration when
applied to an animal or a child, but with irra-
tional distaste when applied to an adult human
being. Two personal experiences come to mind involving perseverance and cunning. I find them
fascinating because in each I was on the opposite
side of the fence, so to speak.

Many years ago, I was an assistant buyer for
a large department store. Buyers develop special
relationships - - - personal and otherwise - - -
with favored resources, and it is very difficult
for a new supplier to "crack" an account like that.

PERSEVERANCE

One young man called on me regularly, every two
weeks for six months, to no avail. He offered
extremely tempting deals and promotions, but I
kept giving inane excuses, because I really didn't
want to cut into the business of a favorite manufacturer who had treated us extremely well over
the years. The young rep kept coming back to dis-
play his company's wares. One day, he told me that
he'd had a dream about me the night before, and he
asked if I would like to hear it. Now it's a very
flattering thing to be told that you lie in someone else's subconscious, so I told him to relate the
dream. He unfolded it thus:

> I dreamt that I was on my rounds in
> Manhattan and was hit by a truck and instantly
> killed. I next found myself entering heaven.
> As I passed through the pearly gates, I became
> aware that I had to move my bowels. This sur-
> prised me, because I didn't think that citizens
> of heaven had to concern themselves with such
> mundane matters once the soul arose and left
> the body in earth. I asked one of the arch-
> angels for directions to the men's room. Once
> there, I was enthralled with the porcelain walls,
> solid gold commodes and sterling silver hardware.
> I was just about to perform my function, when I
> spied your face in the commode. I quickly got
> up, adjusted my clothing and ran back to the
> gates. I told the archangel that I couldn't
> use his facility, because the buyer, Hubert
> Bermont, was in the commode. The archangel
> said to me, "Shit on Bermont. He'll never give
> you an order anyhow."

He got his order. The exquisite inventive-
ness of that story could not go unrewarded.

Another time, the situation was reversed.
It was I who sought to crack a big account. This
buyer, too, had his favored resources, and wouldn't
give my factory's merchandise space on his selling
floor to prove itself. One day a severe blizzard
hit that part of the state. All were warned not
to venture out. Armed with my sample case and a
snow-shovel, I drove the sixty miles to that town
in four and a half hours. When I arrived, the
buyer was alone - - - as I had expected. Neither
customers nor drummers had dared to go out that
day. "You must be some kind of a nut to drive
all the way out here on a day like this," he said.
"Not at all," I answered. "I'm just a sales rep
who wants your account very badly and this was the
only means left to me to prove it to you." I got
my order.

Finally, an apocryphal story involving cunning. Fred Smith, while visiting England, made a
special side-trip to Scotland to buy some glen-
plaid woolen fabric so that he could realize a
dream - - - to have a suit made to order for himself with this marvelous textile. He specifically
purchased two yards over the required amount so
that he would be sure to have more than enough
fabric. He lugged the bolt through U.S. Customs
and paid a heavy duty. The very next day, Fred
Smith visited Harold P. Solomon & Company on the
lower east side of New York City; this custom
tailor had come highly recommended. Mr. Solomon

measured Mr. Smith, measured the fabric, and announced
that there wasn't enough on the bolt to make a suit.
Smith was both frustrated and enraged. "I made it
a point to buy extra yardage," he fumed. "Not
enough," intoned Solomon. "I dragged this stuff
three thousand miles and paid duty besides," Smith
begged. "Not enough." Smith left the shop feeling
totally destroyed. One block down the street, Mr.
Sol Lapidus, custom tailor, motioned Smith to enter.
"That's a beautiful piece of plaid you're carrying
there. I'd like to make a suit of it for you."
"Sorry," said Smith, "I obviously don't have enough
yardage." "It can't hurt to measure," shrugged
Lapidus. After measuring and draping, the tailor
announced, "You have plenty. Come back in two
weeks and your suit will be ready." Two weeks to
the day, Fred Smith was admiring himself in the
mirror of Lapidus' establishment. Just then the
proprietor's eight-year-old boy emerged from the
rear of the shop on his way to school. He, too,
was wearing a suit of the identical glen-plaid
cloth. "Isn't that my fabric your boy is wearing?"
asked Smith. "Yes," said Lapidus. "I hope you
don't mind. I had so much left over that I made a
suit for my son." "I don't mind at all. In fact,
I admire your skill," said Smith. After leaving
the shop, the ecstatic owner of a new custom-made
suit of an imported Scottish wollen couldn't help
but re-enter the establishment of Harold P. Solomon.
"Mr. Solomon," said Smith "your competitor, Mr.
Lapidus down the street, not only made a beautiful

suit for me, but had enough cloth left over to make a suit for his eight-year-old boy. Why did you tell me that there wasn't enough yardage?" "Very simple," replied Solomon. "My boy is fourteen."

Do you love the cunning Mr. Solomon? I'm enchanted with him.

VIII. Interview

VIII. Interview

We are all interviewing and being interviewed every
day of our lives. In a real sense, every encounter
with another person is an interview. As children
coming home from school every day we were interviewed by our parents. We have been interviewed
countless times by school officials before gaining
entrance, by prospective employers, by division
heads, by customers and prospective customers, by
officials of every stripe.

Strange word "interview." If broken down,
it means look between. And that's what we are all
doing all the time, really. Everyone is constantly
trying to find out where everyone else "is at" and
what they are about. "Interviewing" or "looking
between" implies that words themselves don't count
for much. One looks between the words by observ-
ing attitudes, postures, body languages, facial

expressions and moods.

It's the easiest thing in today's world to
eliminate whatever "competition" you may encounter
in any kind of interview: selling, buying, trading,
job-hunting, promoting (yourself or a product) or
negotiating. Just look around and see who is "com-
peting" with you. Look at the passive faces, the
don't-give-a-damn attitudes, the laziness, the
procrastination, the turned-off, tuned-out brains,
the lack of attention. The eminent Krishnamurti
once summed up his entire philosophy of the art of
living in two words: Pay Attention. That's all you
have to do today to shine in our sleepwalking society.
Pay attention. What is the other person really saying? What does he or she really want or need? Can
you satisfy that need? Never mind their exact words.
Look between the words by asking questions: interview. Interview whether you are the interviewer or
the interviewee.

In my half-century of living on this planet,
I guess I have been interviewed formally one hundred times and have interviewed others a thousand
times. I believe this is about average. Most of
the people I interviewed as possible employees
insisted on talking first about salary and next
about fringe benefits. Intelligent questions
about the exact nature of the work itself were
rare. In only four or five instances in all my
executive life did I ever hear "I'd really love to

work here; what do I have to do to get this great
job?" Needless to say, those people were hired
immediately. The others all seemed as though they
couldn't have cared less one way or the other. The
interviewer is dying to be sold a bill of goods;
candidates don't seem to know that. What has always amazed me most is that, considering the fact
that I was the potential employer, *no one* ever asked
me anything personal about myself, despite the
interminable questions of a personal nature that I
asked them.

Well, you might answer by reminding me that
most interviewees are frightened, being in that
uncomfortable "tested" position in the first place.
But this is not 1935. In nine cases out of ten the
employer is far more desperate to fill a position
with a competent and worthwhile employee than is
the candidate desperate for work. (Just compare
the "help wanted" and "positions wanted" ads in
the classified section of your newspaper.) It
doesn't *seem* that way to someone unemployed being
interviewed by someone who is employed. Pay attention. If you are a willing and conscientious person, you are a highly prized and sought-after
commodity in today's job market.

Let's move this subject to sales. The only
really effective method of selling is by paying
attention to your customer's needs in the form of
specific and intelligent questions, i.e. by a pre-

cise interview. Sure, you may sell something once
in a while by the sheer force of your personality
or aggressiveness; but you won't make a long-term
customer or a friend. Furthermore, you will come
home exhausted every day from your constant combat.
You won't make much money, either.

Let me be more graphic about the success and
rewards that come from one person's paying attention amidst a slothful society like the one we live
in today. We need only take a few of the many pages
from Madison Avenue's brilliant notebooks. And we
don't even have to go into things like subliminal
selling as described so well in the book *Media
Sexploitation*. In the early days when a large Coke
was a dime and a small one was a nickel, Coca Cola
was looking to increase its share of market at the
soda fountain. Instead of studying consumer motivation, they studied the lack of it. So the order
went out across the country to stop asking the
patron whether he or she wanted a large or small
Coke; instead, when a Coke was requested, the clerk
was to simply ask "Large?" Most of the responses
were a nod of the head. It was just *too much trouble*
to say, "No, small." The extra nickels added up
to extra millions. People just aren't paying attention out there. I wish I had a five-dollar bill
for every time I ever approached a customer on a
retail floor with the greeting,"Good morning!"
and was answered with,"No, thanks, I'm just looking."
If you keep your eyes and ears open and your mind

alert, how can you possibly fail in a world of
zombies like this? It really doesn't take genius
to come out on top. You need only pay attention.

IX. The Executive Function

IX. The Executive Function

There are all kinds of books on how to become an
effective executive - - - from the excellent works
of Peter Drucker on down. A bibliography of them
would be longer than this book. There are also
books on power, aggression and other such foolish-
ness deemed necessary to become successful in today's business world. Add to this the infinite
variety of courses and seminars given everywhere
and we have an information overload of mammoth
proportions. This chapter assumes that you have
culled what is essential from the aforementioned,
or that, if you haven't as yet, you will do so
soon. (Please refer to the section on rapid
reading in Chapter 4.) Instead, it is my purpose
to set down here some ideas which are not available
elsewhere and/or which you may not have thought of
before. I hope they are as innovative to you now
as they were to me when I discovered them.

First, even setting the biological fallacy aside, there is no such thing as a self-made man. Any successful person who ever tells you that he made it on his own is either lying or suffering from amnesia. Every one who has risen to the top has had teachers, mentors, friends, colleagues and/or superiors who have assisted, supported, shared, invested and/or taught all along the way. Joan Manley, President of Time-Life Books, constantly attributes her success to her first boss (for whom she was secretary), who consistently shared his knowledge with her. I have been in the business world for thirty-two years. Recently, I decided to give a small, informal party for a few people who helped me with two of my projects during the past three years. After going through my wheeldex, I found that *forty-three people* fit that description. Forty of them honored me by attending. When I thanked them for all the assistance they had given me, each of them reminded me that, somewhere along the line, I had helped them in their careers as well. So the way to get help is to give it. I can hear you muttering, "This guy is yelling 'Eureka' for having discovered The Golden Rule." You betcha. And further on, I might even invent the wheel!

* * *

Next, let's talk about making deals. I am constantly amazed at the number of business people I come across who actually believe that the only good deal is the one in which they come out on top - - - or even where they win and the other

party loses. (On the other hand, I did say previously that, as a young, inexperienced salesman
I felt myself to be in such an adversary position,
didn't I?) In every business deal *all* the parties
involved must come out winning; if *any* party loses,
you will ultimately lose, too. This is a hard-and-
fast rule. The other party, if injured in any way,
will either exact retribution some day or will not
live up to his or her end of the agreement, and
this usually results in litigation. Additionally,
the ill-will, bad feelings and needless physical
and emotional energy spent (not to mention the
money) are never worth it. In a good deal everyone must be satisfied; and this doesn't always
mean monetarily. A good dealer determines well in
advance what it really is that the other person
wants. It could be sales volume, profits, stock,
security, prestige, a tax shelter, friendship, or,
of course, money - - - or any combination of these
things. Strangely, this needs to be said, too:
you must also analyze your own motives in advance.
Otherwise, a lack of definite purpose on your part
could easily lead to your being "touted off" during
the negotiations.

Remember J. Paul Getty and his constant aware-
ness of his own goal; he was never deflected during
any of his negotiations. I am a consultant, and I
once found myself with a client, engaged in the
following discussion:

He: My company has shown no real growth in three

years. Can you help me?

Me: Tell me about your company.

He: It's a fine organization. I started it seven
years ago in my small New England home town.
I have the best people working for me and
they are all my friends. We have shown a
net profit after salaries and taxes every
year. Most importantly, we have established
ourselves nationally as the very best in the
business. This is due to constant investment
in the latest equipment and the skill with
which we work in our quiet and friendly atmos-
phere. But when it comes to growth, the company doesn't seem to be getting anywhere.

Me: What's your problem?

He: I beg your pardon?

Me: You have described a most idyllic situation.
Your very tone of voice and facial expressions
bespeak pride in your company and its accom-
plishments. Moreover, you are obviously the
most contented person I have seen in my office
in years. It has probably occurred to you
more than once that you could increase your
volume by a large and expensive advertising
campaign, thereby requiring more skilled
help than your small town can supply; this
would cut down on your excellent performance
level. It has also undoubtedly crossed your
mind - - - you impress me as a highly intelli-

gent man - - - that you can capture a
larger share of the market by moving your
company to New York or Chicago. But your
pleasant life-style and peaceful ways of
doing business would be disrupted, and you
would lose many of your employees who are
your friends. What is your real goal in
life?

He: You can't imagine how foolish I feel, never
to have given my own personal goal that much
thought. All I hear and read about in the
business world is the importance of "growth,"
and I felt that we were deficient in that
area. My goal, of course, is to continue
to enjoy my company, my life-style and my
work-style as long as I can. At the moment,
I cannot see that any of these things are
in jeopardy. You are correct. I have no
problem.

The important thing about this client is that, without this kind of self-analysis of his own situation,
he was in a perfect position to be "plucked" in
some possible merger deal by someone else who really
understood himself.

* * *

Let's move on. We learn, as we grow older,
that there are no such things as totally good guys
and totally bad guys; real people are made up of
the many shades of gray in between. But there

are total winners and total losers in the business and professional world. To call someone *somewhat* of a winner or loser is akin to saying that a woman is *somewhat* pregnant. She either is or she isn't. A winner is a winner and a loser is a loser. Also, sportsmanship aside, there is no such thing as "a good loser." A *good* loser is a *real* loser. The point is that associating with losers is the biggest waste of your time imaginable, and you need this valuable time to reach your own goals. Conversely, associating with winners will smooth your course immeasurably. Who are these winners and losers, and how do we identify them? First, it goes without saying that there are ten times as many losers as there are winners. So, losers, being much more in evidence, are in a much better position to make contact with you, mix it up with you, and waste your time. They can be spotted by the following characteristics:

a) A fawning, ingratiating, over-complimenting attitude.

b) A placement of high priority on faddish image with regard to clothes, cars, restaurants, Muzak and youth.

c) The presentation of ideas, concepts and deals which have not been properly thought through.

d) A lack of time and constant pressure of being harried and hurried.

e) A lack of substance in the products they make or the services they render.

f) An inability to stick to the point of any conversation.

g) A need to begin every sentence with such phrases as: "To be perfectly frank," "To tell you the truth," "I can state with total candor," "I sincerely believe," etc.

h) A need to attempt to brighten his or her own light by diminishing someone else's (which can't be done).

And the winners? They are simply people who exhibit characteristics exactly opposite of those described above. I wish I could recoup the time (and money) I have lost by getting involved in nonsensical projects proposed by losers. Some losers are nice people. Some are my friends. But friendship is one thing and business is another.

* * *

Most people are so pre-occupied with trouble-shooting and fixing whatever is wrong with their organizations that they forget to contemplate and analyze what is right. What's right is just as important as what's wrong. Understanding what is right can make you successfully expand and make you expend more time, effort and money in that direction. What is wrong merely has to be stopped. The new opportunities for your business or profession lie in the area of what is going well for

you. And *the recognition and seizing of an opportunity
is the primary talent inherent in a good executive or businessman.* We cannot specifically plan our entire
careers. Opportune things happen out there which
create a set of circumstances calling upon us to
seize the day and act. It is our recognition of
this and our action which prohibits calling a new
venture into which we enter through the back door
an "accident." In this sense, nothing in life is
accidental.

* * *

So we cannot plan our careers. But we *can*
plan our days. Ben Franklin advised us to plan a
set of things to do each day and to be certain that
the day doesn't end until we have accomplished these
tasks. Losers don't plan their days. Most executives I know experience a "shit-hit-the-fan" kind
of day. They enter their places of business all
psyched up to merely handle whatever problems come
up. By the time they have taken care of the last
problem of the day, they are too exhausted for anything that is creative, educational or fun. These
people are in no emotional state to recognize any
opportunity much less to seize one. Your day is
yours, not *theirs.* So is your life, for that matter.

* * *

Murphy's "Law" (whatever can go wrong will)
is utter nonsense. It is a palliative for the
passive person. The *active* person sees to it that
things do *not* go wrong. Sure, sometimes you depend

on other people and other organizations to get
things done and sometimes they goof. But what
then? Most people I know, in a circumstance like
this, do one of two things. They either pray very
hard that the problem will go away or they pray
even harder that the customer either won't notice
it or won't do anything about it. Prayers like
these are never answered. I'm sure that the people
at the Ford Motor Company prayed very hard that no
one would notice that the Pinto's rear section was
a potential human furnace. And the people at General Motors prayed just as hard that the Oldsmobile
customer wouldn't notice that his car had a Chevrolet engine. No. You avoid problems by calling them
to your customers' (or clients') attention before
they call them to yours. That's the way to de-fuse
a complaint - - - by letting the customer know up
front that you care, deeply. _Do_ you care deeply?
If not, you really have no basis for being in business.

* * *

There is another side to this coin. What
about when you are in the right? Do you fight for
that right? Or do you cave in, avoid "getting
involved" and "go along?" This, too, is terribly
important for your self-respect. The amount of
business or money involved is unimportant. When
you're right, you're right! I have spent what
others would consider to be inordinate amounts of
time fighting anyone and everyone who I felt were

trying to take advantage of me. The matter of right
and wrong is obviously more important to me than to
my adversaries, because they refuse to expend as
much effort in these matters as I do - - - so I win.
But it's the attendant feelings of exhilaration
that count for me. Dammit, they are wrong, and I
can't let them win because of my own negligence.

But be sure you're right!

* * *

There is something else I haven't found in
books or articles about business, i.e. the proper
use of an outside professional, expert or consultant. Whenever you retain the services of a professional of any kind, be certain of two things:

1. That you have hired the best in the busi-
    ness. Check other clients and references
    thoroughly.

2. That you never attempt to second-guess him
    in his own field.

It is this second rule I'd like to discuss with you
by way of several examples.

I once found myself on the set of a fashion
photography session. In attendance were the model,
a famous photographer and the dress manufacturer
who was paying the tab. As the photographer was
getting ready to shoot, the manufacturer inter-
rupted by asking what lens opening he was using.

The question was prefaced by the fact that the manufacturer owned a Nikon like the one in use and so he knew something about it. Well, if looks could kill - - -. The photographer froze for a few moments, then turned and walked out of the room, never to return.

The success story of the original Volkswagen Beetle in this country is now legendary. We also know that this triumph was due primarily to the most effective advertising campaign ever launched. You will recall that the car itself was not only unknown here, but was considered quite ugly. But I once read about how that campaign originated. A small advertising agency, with nothing to lose, insisted that it be given total *carte blanche* concerning the actual ads. VW was to control the budget only, not any part of the creative advertising process. Indeed, the client was to have absolutely no say in the latter at all. Strangely enough, the German firm (much to its credit) accepted this arrangement. The results are history. I've always felt that, of all the service fields, I would be least amenable to entering advertising. *Everybody* thinks he knows something about advertising, and every amateur will argue with a professional. The VW story is rare. Most often, we are witness to hodge-podge advertising campaigns which are obviously compromises geared to satisfy a number of different committees at variance with each other's interests and with the ultimate sales of the product.

Ever try to convince an automobile salesman that you know something about cars when you really don't? Tire-kicking, peering under the hood and even those things suggested by "Consumer's Guide" don't fool the salesman for a moment. You would fare much better if you admitted that you know nothing and placed him on his honor. The other way he is ready to do combat with you in the certain knowledge that you are a push-over. I once owned a furniture store which specialized in bedding. Now, a mattress, despite the labelling regulations, is really a "blind" item. Only the dealer and manu- facturer actually know the internal construction. It used to tickle me to see customers shove their knees into a mattress (which amounts to the same thing as kicking a tire) and ask questions about how many coils the mattress contained. (It's not the coil-count that is important but how the coils are tied.) These customers never got the best value, because they never asked for it. They only showed off with their misinformation. But, once in a while, a customer would come in and say to me, "We are look- ing for a youth mattress for our seven-year-old. We were told that it is important for the proper devel- opment of her spine to get her something good. We know nothing about mattresses. What can you suggest?" Those people were putting me on my honor and my met- tle. They were making *me* responsible for their child's health. I couldn't in good conscience sell them something inferior. I bent over backwards to help them in every way. They invariably got the best deals.

Put the expert on his honor. Let him do his thing. Don't compete with him in his own field. Only losers do that.

* * *

Finally, we must indeed invent the wheel here. With regard to any given project you are working on, are you doing absolutely everything that can possibly be done to make it succeed? Have you omitted anything? Have you forgotten anything? Have you neglected anything? Wouldn't it be terrible if the project failed and two years from now you were to sit bolt upright in bed at two in the morning in a cold sweat saying to yourself, "I'll bet that if I had gotten on a plane and visited Stan Jones in Houston, that project would have hit. Maybe even just a phone call to Stan - - -." Better to know now and forever that if a project fails it does so in spite of the fact that you have done everything humanly possible in its behalf. It takes a lot of the sting out of the failure. It is easier to accept the fact that you might be wrong than the fact that you are lazy or slipshod. Here again, if you're going to strike out, you might as well strike out swinging.

X. The Businessman As Cop

X. The Businessman As Cop

At least once a month, we find, buried on a back
page of the financial section of the newspaper, an
article on white-collar crime. The billions lost
to business mount exponentially each year. The
reason for this outrageous increase is that the
perpetrators of these crimes are rarely adequately
punished; this, in turn, encourages more such crime.
And the reason for this lack of justice is two-fold.

a) These crimes are not classified as violent.

b) The perpetrators are generally in the upper
echelons of society, and we do indeed have
a two-tiered system of justice.

But these crimes *are* violent. They do violence to
our entire system of economics and to our sense of
ethics. Moreover, they comprise one of the leading
causes of our terrible inflation. White-collar
crime is rape. And rape is a violent crime. In
all legal transactions, a corporation is treated as

a person. This "person" is being raped every day
everywhere in the country.

What gets the most publicity, on the other
hand, is shop-lifting. Shop-lifting accumulates
to a fairly high price, too, but absolutely nothing
as compared to *internal* theft. External theft is
retail theft. Internal theft is wholesale theft.
Employees steal more than customers. This is a well-
known but unpublicized fact.

So two of the most important but distasteful
roles of the executive are those of detective and
enforcer. But, because they *are* so unsavory, most
executives prefer not to assume them. As the saying goes, these businessmen have eyes but they see
not and they have ears but they hear not. Despite
the fact that they usually secretly suspect a number
of incidents of wrongdoing on the part of new and
even old-time employees, these executives simply
cannot bring themselves to investigate them. They
remind me of the man who was hit by a truck and was
spied a few minutes later furtively trying to crawl
away from the scene of the accident; he explained
that he didn't want to get involved.

What *is* white-collar crime? How big must the
theft be to be labelled as such? Why is it so much
more prevalent now than heretofore? It seems to me
that what is currently being called the age of the
new morality should be named the age of the new
immorality. Our government has been trying so hard

to become socialistic by endless legislation to re-distribute the wealth that the populace has pre-empted Congress by deciding to help it along in illegally conducting this re-distribution on its own. The concept of private property diminishes daily. A few years ago, for example, some youngsters put this to the test by camping on exclusive, privately-owned beach property which had been dearly paid for by the homeowners who had deeds to it. The local government, to avoid a confrontation, ruled that the shoreline itself was public property. So too, the employee guiltlessly robs the "impersonal" corporation. Merchandise, office supplies, cleaning equipment and supplies, light bulbs, toilet paper, postage, money, expense accounts - - - it makes no difference. There seems to be *so much of it* around. What harm if some of it is taken? Who will miss it? Aside from the fact that these criminals (yes stealing two rolls of toilet paper is a criminal act) are stupid because they are unable to tie the company's health to their own earnings, they are also immoral. Once, many years ago, a former employee at R.H. Macy was caught stealing thousands of dollars from the pneumatic cash-tubes in use at that time. Guess what he had done with the money; he had bought shares of Macy stock!

What is the actual difference between an office clerk who deliberately and knowingly steals ten dollars worth of your office supplies for his home use and the comptroller who embezzles ten thousand dollars from your company till? There is no difference.

THE BUSINESSMAN AS COP

Are you as vigilant as you should be? Do you think enough about things like this? Do you thoroughly check out the references of potential new employees - - - particularly when you are desparate for help? Do you periodically check the credit references of your staff to learn whether or not they are in personal financial difficulty? Do you thoroughly check out rumors concerning theft, even though you think they are falsely and maliciously started? Do you have employees who are really your "partners" unbeknownst to you? In short, do you care enough about your business to protect it?

XI. The Market

XI. The Market

There is an old saying which goes, "Build a better mousetrap, and the world will beat a path to your door." Maybe that was true generations ago, but it isn't true in today's business arena. Now we would have to change it to, "Build a better mouse-trap, and five other companies will try to knock you off in short order." Too many businessmen still try to make minor improvements on what they produce in order to increase their share of market, instead of coming up with something entirely new in their field in order to capture *all* of an entirely *new* market. Once again, the automobile industry is a perfect example. (I'm grateful to it for giving me so much to write about.) Detroit has been fooling around and tinkering with its cars for years and years - - - adding a strip of chrome here or a new grill there. But twice now Volkswagen has introduced completely new and differ-

ent cars; first the Bug and now the Rabbit.
Shazzam! They walk away with all the marbles.
Then they stay light-years ahead by putting a
diesel engine into a compact car, while Detroit
tries to keep up from light-years behind. Go for
all of the market, not just a share of it.

It's easier to capture a new market today
than it used to be. What's required is an innovative turn of mind. We live in an affluent,
materialistic, faddish society of almost 220
million people. Come up with anything specialized
that is useful, aesthetic and/or fun, address the
appropriate specialized market, and you'll have it
all. There are thousands of such success stories
that sprang from imaginative, creative minds which
understood the consumer psyche - - - from the Pet
Rock to MacDonald's to the Rabbit. Why keep knock-
ing your brains out twenty-four hours a day just
to stay one millimeter ahead of your nearest competitor? If you already have a fairly successful
business going, use a little bit of your profits
to come up with something entirely new. If you
are just starting out, start right with innovation.

We live in an age of extreme specialization.
Forty years ago, it would have been inconceivable
for a merchant to make a living by opening a shop
which sold slacks exclusively. Today, a specialty
shop can make it by selling only *denim* slacks.
The general store is out; the specialty store is

in. Take another field. Regional book publishing
is now on the rise. Publishing firms are doing
well just producing books about Vermont, let us
say, or just putting out organic gardening books
which deal with a small geographic area. In another vein, it used to be the general cookbook
that was all the rage. Now it's the Italian cookbook, the Jewish cookbook, the Oriental cookbook,
and even the Vietnamese cookbook. The general
magazine has fallen on hard times, too. Gone are
The Saturday Evening Post, Liberty, and others of the
same ilk. So the moguls have switched to producing *Money, People, Body Building,* etc. Carry this
to its logical extension with a massive, affluent,
variegated population like ours, and we have the
success of the specialized newsletter. There is
even a newsletter about newsletter publishing!

Share of market? No. *All* of it.

XII. Profits

XII. Profits

In the area of mark-up and profits, I find that
there are two kinds of businessmen: creative entrepreneurs and slide-rule mentalities. The
slide-rule person sets the same mark-up and profit
margin on his entire line, regardless of the desir-
ability, the exclusivity, the saleability or the
value of each of the items. The entrepreneur
charges whatever he believes the traffic will
bear; he throws the slide-rule away in the full
knowledge that ofttimes the cost of anything has
no relationship to its market value. (Look at
real estate.)

"What?" screams the enraged government bureau-
crat. "Are you advocating excessive unconscionable
profits in our inflationary economy?" Believe me,
no one in Washington I ever spoke with has ever
been able to define "excessive" or "unconscionable"

with regard to profits. Whose conscience are they
referring to? Theirs? They have less conscience
than any other sector of our society. If advocacy
it is, then I am advocating getting the most profit possible from any business you transact. If
you are in a competitive situation, your competition
will set the bounds of your profit. If you are not
in a competitive situation, your market will put
some kind of a limit on your price. (Let's face
it, we have been mindlessly tooling around in our
cars all these years because gasoline has been so
cheap.) So there is no such thing as unconscionable or excessive profits. The consumer society
itself places a limit on all prices - - - except
in the non-competitive areas of monopolistic uti-
lities (wholeheartedly supported by the government.)
The government can't and shouldn't place those lim-
its. Price-fixing doesn't work, makes people cheat,
creates shortages due to less profitable production,
and causes general mayhem.

We don't need examples, but I'll offer a simple one here, anyhow. I recently required a foam
rubber pad to put under my electric typewriter in
order to cut down on the clatter. I went to my
regular office-supply store one block from my office. They had it in stock, as they do most things.
The price was $4.95. We are talking about a raw
piece of foam rubber, one-quarter of an inch thick,
which couldn't possibly cost more than forty cents
to manufacture and cut. But I paid it! I wanted

and needed that item then and there. I had neither the time nor the inclination to go to a department store and have them cut a piece of foam rubber for me which would have done the job at less than half the price. So the $4.95 was appropriate, regardless of the high profit. Good for them! How high could they go? Well, at eight dollars I would have withstood my typewriter clatter a while longer and they would have lost a sale. I'm still waiting for someone to explain to me how any of this is the government's business.

Joseph Heller wrote a marvelous novel called *Good As Gold*. In it, he ridicules White House doublespeak. He has an official saying things like "I thought of calling you all day, but it never entered my mind." Or, "We haven't come up with any ideas yet, but I assure you that they are very concrete." Well, it's to laugh, but the fact that they really talk this way is sad, disturbing, confusing and infuriating. Right now the administration is taking the business world to task for "excessive" profits on the one hand, and assuming credit for the upward movement of the economic indicators on the other hand. COME ON! This is an administration? If you had an "administration" like that in your organization, you would have been bankrupt and out of business long ago. The government *is* bankrupt; it just keeps doing business - - - if we can call it that.

XIII. Advertising And Presentation

XIII. Advertising And Presentation

I can hear you muttering again. "This guy bemoans
the fact that every Tom, Dick and Harry thinks he
is an advertising man, and now he is going to stick
us with his own unprofessional two-cents worth."
In a sense, but not really.

I would first like to remind you to retain
the services of the very best advertising professionals you can find, and then remind you not to
second-guess them. The agency that can't find anything wonderful about whatever it is you are selling
is the wrong agency. Sometimes these advertising
slogans have nothing at all to say, so they say
nothing at all. "It takes a lot of nerve to call
a beer Old Milwaukee." Yessir, it certainly does.
But aside from the fact that we are dealing with a
pretty nervy company, how good is the beer? Here's
another. "Sure, there are lots of investment firms,

but there's only one Merrill, Lynch." What does
that tell us? At the time that slogan appeared
there was also only one Idi Amin and there were
only two giant pandas at the National Zoo. Let's
not forget that these companies are spending for-
tunes of money to *motivate* us. Again, it insults
our intelligence to tell us that we can't tell a
Mercury from a Mercedes. The last person to con-
fuse them suffered from the final stages of glau-
coma. A good advertising slogan? "Volkswagen
does it again," as indeed it *has*.

(As an aside, I must confess that I have never
bought, nor would I ever buy a Mercedes or a Volkswagen. I simply have an unremitting prejudice a-
gainst a country that can produce a holocaust. But
I do admire their craftsmanship, resourcefulness
and business acumen.)

In our constant quest for the eternal "hype,"
we seem to have lost sight of an old, old advertising truism. The very best advertisement is a sale,
which thereby puts another of your products or services out there for people to notice, admire and
recommend by word-of-mouth. It is also the least
expensive. This assumes, of course, that you are
engaged in producing something worthwhile.

Another very important principle of advertising is the constant attention to the reduction of
risk. If you are a flamboyant high-roller, you

belong at the nearest *chemin-de-fer* table, but not in business. It is a well-established fact that advertising is *initially* the biggest crap-shoot of all. The race track is safer; at least there are never more than eleven horses (variables) in a race. The number of variables in even the smallest advertising campaign is infinite - - - from the many media to the artwork, size, wording and even typeface. Many's the businessman who has been forced into bankruptcy by faulty or over-extended advertising. This, despite such "scientific" tools as consumer motivation research and advance surveys; these are all bunk. *"Would* you buy?" is never the same as *"Will* you buy?"

Notice that the word "initially" was used above. When and if an ad *does* pull, the crap-shoot is over, and the art of riding it for all it is worth comes to the fore. This art consists of two "skills":

1. Never changing the smallest detail of that ad, no matter how strongly you think (or know) that you can improve upon it. The infinite variety and number of imponderable variables have come together to mystically (yes, *mystically*) work for you and should not be tampered with in any way. Sometimes, your professional experts may advise otherwise in order to justify additional fees. Don't listen to them

this one time.

2. Keeping accurate and detailed records of
    your results so that you will know exact-
    ly when your campaign is starting to reach
    the public's saturation point. In this
    way, you can terminate it before losing
    some of the profits the campaign has
    earned.

One more point about reducing the enormous risks
of advertising. Free advertising, or publicity,
is better than paid advertising. First, because
it costs less, and second, because it pulls better.
Someone else blowing your horn always get more
customer reaction than you blowing your own. So,
ofttimes, the services of a top-notch public relations firm can bring in more business less ex-
pensively than the services of an advertising agency.
However, both, working in concert, is always the best
possible arrangement - - - if you can afford it.

With regard to presentation, I must, once a-
gain, define my terms. I equate presentation with
the packaging of the product or service. I do *not*
mean the institutional image of your company as it
relates to high rents, awe-inspiring architecture,
out-of-sight furnishings and interior decoration,
gorgeous receptionists, sexy lighting or instant
music on the telephone wire when the customer is
put on "hold." All of these things are not only
wasteful, but forewarn the public that it is paying
too much for whatever it is you are selling, i.e.

they actually *hurt* your business.

Packaging today *is* a science, and we have highly skilled graphics experts who know how to put it
into practice; indeed, we have some of the best in
the world. It is possible to make beer, cereal,
hosiery, books and other products literally leap
off the shelves by designing bottles, cans, boxes
and jackets which are either inviting to the touch
and/or aesthetically lovely to behold.

Again, we live in the most affluent society
on earth. We can afford to (and will) spend on
packaging which appeals to our eye, our intellect,
our fantasy and even our whim. I once took part
in a merchandising campaign of sculpture museum
reproductions. Each piece was accompanied by a
printed "legend" which described its source and
"authenticity" in detail. Although the replicas
were skillfully and exquisitely crafted, they could
never have sold without the accompanying legend.
In effect, we were *giving away* the sculpture and
selling the romance. That is presentation in its
highest form. Can't you apply this to your business? Another even more successful example of
this principle (albeit a ludicrous one) was the
Pet Rock. The rock itself, of course, was super-
fluous. The small box with the "air" holes was
much more of an attraction. But the little pam-
phlet (which probably cost a penny) explaining in
detail the care and feeding of the rock, was the

clincher; without it, the entire merchandising
scheme would have failed. The importance of
presentation cannot be overestimated.

XIV. Favors, Commissions, Gifts, Kick-Backs & Pay-Offs

XIV. Favors, Commissions, Gifts, Kick-Backs & Pay-Offs

The government doesn't understand business. This
is as it should be; it isn't expected of government to understand because business is none of
its business. There should be as much separation
between Business and State as there is between
Church and State. But there isn't. Time and
again, the state has entered into the business
world with disastrous results. The government
knows neither how to buy, how to sell nor how to
manage. When it comes to buying anything, it pays
too much; witness the Pentagon or the General Services Administration. When it comes to selling
anything, it charges too little; witness its sur-
plus sales and the Government Printing Office.
When it comes to managing any enterprise, witness
a hotel in Washington called Harambee House, built
to aid minority enterprises with ten million dollars of government money; in short order, there

were missing funds, unpaid bills, lawsuits, etc.
Since these government "enterprises" are bank-
ruptcy-proof with unlimited taxpayer money, they
keep operating - - - often in direct competition
with private businesses which run every risk of
bankruptcy. Unfair, of course, but there it is.

Then comes the injurious further insult when
government tells private enterprise how to do business, and how not to. We now have legislation
which makes it a crime to pay someone off in order
to make a sale, and a crime to accept such a pay-
off. Everything from a large sum of money to a
two-martini lunch has been banned. Bad enough
that the State knows nothing about the creative
art of selling; it now prohibits us from prac-
ticing that art.

What's so creative about pay-offs? Ever try
it? You must know, who, when, where and how much.
You must also know your competition, because every
one else is attempting it. It's not easy. There is
an obvious exception. Under no circumstances can
one condone the attempted bribe of a government
official, whose mandate it is to act solely for the
public good. We are dealing here only with attempted
transactions within the private sector. We have
legislated ourselves out of the international market with these rules, while France, Germany, Japan
and others simply go in and pick up that business;
our entrepreneurs simply stand around with their

hands tied behind their backs. Where does the government draw these lines, and how far will it go?

Consider. During World War II, there were all kinds of shortages - - - accompanied by price controls. It is endemic to human nature to circumvent controls of any kind, and all kinds of ingenuity is brought to bear on the attempt. People wanted their scotch wiskey. It was in low supply. Business couldn't do the natural thing by raising the price. So the distributors forced the dealers to take two cases of gin (not in demand) with each case of scotch; the dealer, in turn, passed this method of merchandising along to the retail customer. Business continued unabated. People "learned" (in a Pavlovian way) to enjoy gin. Such is the primal economic law of supply and demand, which the government continuously tries to usurp. To quote Kurt Vonnegut, "And so it goes."

In the early part of this book we discussed the difficulty of cracking a new account. Businessmen create and establish close working relationships with each other, just like anyone else. Indeed, some of these relationships become close friendships. *Favors* are exchanged, which make the wheels of industry and mercantilism turn much more easily and smoothly. I could cite a zillion examples, but here are just a few:

a) A buyer tells a long-time favored supplier that he needs a special promotion to stay alive. To keep the account, the manufacturer offers the merchandise at cost this one time. (There is a law against this.)

b) A manufacturer is in difficulty. He has a temporary cash-flow problem and cannot meet his payroll. He asks a favored customer to pre-pay some invoices. The customer complies.

c) In appreciation for contributing towards an excellent, profitable year, one businessman will send his best customer a calendar, another will send a case of liquor, another will send a season box at the opera, and another might send a new car. To reject any of these well-deserved gifts would be both improper and impolite. (But there is a law against this, too.)

d) Conversely, in appreciation for contributing towards an excellent year, a *customer* may reward a *supplier* with additional business the following year by taking it away from other suppliers which weren't quite so accommodating.

And so on. What amateurs fail to realize is that in this competitive world, it isn't *always* price

and quality alone which win the day. Businessmen
are esentially people who follow the rules of
fair-play. They respond to a favor with "I owe
you one." Conversely, they respond to a hosing
with "You'll get yours for this." These "ledgers"
are kept meticulously. Also, most favors cannot
be equated with exact amounts of money. If a printer
clears his presses so that one favored publisher
gets his book out on time, how much is that worth?
And if a customer always pays his bills within thirty days so that the supplier can _count_ on it, how
much is _that_ worth? (Don't forget how Mr. Brown
became assistant to the president in Chapter 1.)

No, no, says government. There can be no
favoritism in business. Really? And when, through
the _legal_ system of pork-barreling, friends get big
government jobs because they previously did _political_
favors, what's that? What kind of double standard
is this?

Recently, the Internal Revenue Service dis-
allowed the deduction of a business lunch on the
grounds that the guest was an old-time consistent
customer and no business had been transacted _as a
direct result of that particular lunch._ What was the
businessman supposed to do - - - let his competitor start taking his customer to lunch?

If we aren't careful, the State will condemn
selling by merely regulating it out of existence.

FAVORS, GIFTS, ETC.

Then we can *all* stay at home.

I know that what we are espousing here is unpopular. But this book didn't set out to win .ny popularity contest.

XV. Money

XV. Money

We move now from the unpopular to the totally
outrageous. There has been a monetary philosophy
abroad in this land for the past forty years which
was conceived by the government, promulgated by
the economists and sold to us by the accountants.
That philosophy encompasses two commandments:

    I   Thou shalt not save.

    II Thou shalt spend more than thine earnings.

As for the government, we have dealt with its wis-
dom before, but just to focus on this illuminated
ivory tower in the area of economics, consider:

- It passes a regulation to alleviate the
  energy crisis. Oil from an old well shall
  bring a maximum price of $5 per barrel;
  oil from a new well can bring a price of
  $11 per barrel. Presto! Through sheer
  alchemy the government turns honest oil-

men into lawbreakers. They simply call
old oil new oil. Wouldn't you?

- The non-discriminating government allows
  grants and loans for every type of under-
  taking except one - - - *publishing*.

- The government managed to increase its
  regulations from 20,000 pages in 1970 to
  61,000 pages in 1978.

- ICC, FAA and FTC regulations have elimi-
  nated most of the competition from hundreds
  of industries, thereby creating the leading
  cause of high prices and contributing most
  to our inflation.

- In 1977 alone, regulatory agencies cost
  forty-eight major corporations 2.6 billion
  dollars.

- Under the guise of trying to eliminate high
  unemployment, the anti-discrimination government will give huge loans to large corporations in trouble to prevent their bank-
  ruptcies (Pan-Am to mind), but would do
  nothing to help prevent your bankruptcy
  or mine.

Let us turn now to the disciples, the economists. Never in our history has a group of "experts"
been so wrong for so long a time, with the possible
exception of the weather forecasters. Not only are
they and their theories forever wrong, but they have
a peculiar, inverted way of looking at things.

David Broder put it this way: "In the perverse
world of the economic planners, a boost in profits or a reduction in unemployment means the
economy is overheating - - - not that someone
is making money or finding a job." But, of course,
they go on theorizing and planning to prevent *themselves* from becoming an unemployment statistic.

Moving closer to home (us), we have our
accountants, financial advisers and/or brokers.
What's their message from "on high?" Simply this:

- Get rid of your money. It will do you no
  good in a savings bank, because the inflation will soon eat it away.

- If you don't unload your money *somehow,* the
  government will get it in taxes, because
  you will show too much profit.

- Whatever you spend costs you only 60%-70%
  of the price, because, as business deduc-
  tions, the government really picks up the
  rest of the tab. So spend, spend, spend.
  Keep that money in circulation.

- Don't pay bills promptly. Hold off as long
  as you possibly can. Use that money in the
  interim for investment.

- Keep a keen eye on your cash-flow situation
  by proper use of charts, projections and,
  where necessary, computers. But always
  make sure that the money flows out as fast
  as it flows in.

- Never use your own money; always borrow and deduct the interest.

Most businessmen I know try to follow this a-mazing credo as closely as possible. I'm the only one I know who attempts to do the exact opposite. As a result, they are all wealthier than I am on paper, whereas whatever I have is "tied up in cash."

So, I make my decisions on the spot with the full knowledge that my resources are fluid and at hand. My friends, on the other hand, need time to raise money by selling something, converting some-thing, or borrowing. (And this time is usually costly.) By paying all of my bills *immediately* I have wonderful peace of mind, I am never harassed by creditors, and my suppliers bend over backwards to treat me well (as you can imagine). My friends always seem to be under a strain, are constantly hounded by bill-collectors and fight incessantly with their suppliers - - - changing them often.

The concept of borrowing rather than saving and using your own money has had me baffled for years. I sometimes feel like the only sane per-son in a nuthouse - - - but then I remember that every truly *insane* person feels that way. Let's take a simple illustration. I'll assume that you, like I, are not entitled to the prime rate of in-terest. At the risk of outdating this book (in-terest rates fluctuating as they do), let's suppose that we have $10,000 which is in a normal savings account drawing 6% interest. Rather than use this money, we follow the experts' advice and borrow $10,000 for business purposes from the bank at 15% interest. Yes, the $1,500 interest is deductible, which means that if our company is in the 33% bracket, the loan only cost us $1,000. But using our own money would have cost us $600 (the lost in-interest on our savings). Not only that, but with our own money, we have full use of the $10,000 for the entire year, whereas with the loan we only have the use of $8,500. Further, if things don't go *exactly* as planned for the year in question, we are in no trouble at all with our own money, but the bank can foreclose or force re-financing, which costs even more. An over-simplification? Hardly. Finance people deliberately complicate things so that we won't understand them and they can keep collecting fees for all kinds of mystical mumbo jumbo. Notice that - - - as the comic magician said - - - at no time did my fingers leave my hands. (Americans are so used to borrowing that the average family spends nearly 25% of its after-tax income on debt services!)

By paying bills promptly and having more than a sufficient cash reserve on hand, I require no cash-flow charts, projections or computers. This annual savings alone in time and money pays for my vacations. My friends are up to their eyeballs in charts and projections. They take the vacations, too, but not "free" ones like mine.

Inflation does not eat up savings. This is
a myth to make the fool soon parted from his money.
The interest on short-term U.S. Treasury notes
usually keeps up with the inflation rate very well.
"Remember," we are constantly warned, "what happened in Germany in the twenties. People had to go to
the bakery with a wheel-barrow full of money to buy
a loaf of bread." Even if that story were not
apocryphal, we must consider what happened to those
who didn't have the wheel-barrow full of money:
they starved to death. The eminent economist, Milton
Berle, was right: Rich or poor, it's good to have
money.

What does it really mean when we are told
that the I.R.S. picks up a goodly part of our
profligate expenditures when we deduct them? The
I.R.S. actually pays for nothing. It is our fel-
low citizens who pay for our impetuousness - - -
and that's not fair.

Now let's try to handle the big one: TAXES.
There are all kinds of books, newsletters, seminars, articles and experts telling us about tax
evasion, tax avoidance and tax deferrals. Tax
evasion, of course, is against the law, so that
takes care of that. Every plan of tax avoidance
that has ever been presented to me required an
investment so large that it would have made me

paper-rich like my friends, but would have hurt
my method of doing business as described above
and worried me sick as I told you in Chapter 5.
I thought I had come up with the right solution
by purchasing municipal bonds, the interest on
which is totally tax-free. However, this, too,
not only ties up a bunch of capital, but fluct-
uates in value like a faulty speedometer needle,
so that one can lose as easily as one can win
when it comes time to cash in. That leaves tax
deferrals - - - the most ridiculous concept of
all. The theory is that you do not pay taxes now
in your earning prime, but pay them later when
you are older and no longer capable of earning so
much. First, there is no reason to suppose that
at any arbitrary age your earning capacity will
cease or diminish, unless you are the most devout
of pessimists or eat actuarial charts for break-
fast. Second, it seems so foolish to bet against
yourself this way, when your very survival as a
human being requires that you stay in the saddle
as long as you can. (More about this in the last
chapter.) Third, you would lose anyhow because of
the continuous inflationary rise of taxes, i.e. the
tax you pay ten, fifteen or twenty years from now
on this money will be so much more than what you
would pay today, that you will lose even more. *But
nobody ever mentions this.* Break your head all you
want to, you're going to have to pay taxes. As
they say, they are as inevitable as death.

XVI. Your Business Is Your Friend

XVI. Your Business Is Your Friend

We turn now to the other side of money, i.e. its characteristics as life-blood and total nutrition of your business. As such, money in business is not to be played with, fooled with, treated with profligacy or gambled with. Your business should be treated almost as you would treat another human being - - - as a friend. And friend it is. It supplies you and your family with your earnings, it sustains you with a lifelong sense of purpose and career, and it contributes enormously to your society by way of money, goods and direct or in-direct employment. So don't bleed it or milk it.

There are two ways that your business can have money. One way is to earn it. The other way is not to spend it. If your business can do both, it will wind up with twice as much. Elizabeth Seton once advised: "Live simply so that others may simply

live." That is both true and noble. But you
should keep your working life simple so that *you*
may simply live another day. As a businessman,
your income is neither guaranteed nor steady. Nor
is your good health assured forever. (Don't talk
to me about health insurance. I've checked out
that ploy, too; to receive anywhere near your
present income in case of illness requires a pre-
mium equivalent to your right arm and left ventri-
cle.) Not spending profligately nor taxing your
business inordinately because of personal desires
for needless luxuries give you the ultimate lux-
ury: peace of mind and the assurance that you will
always have a business. In this regard, pay heed
to the most important thing that Henry David Thoreau ever said: "A man is as rich as the sum of
the things he can do without."

This sounds like a brief for penury, but it's
not. There is a big difference between *spending*
and *investing,* regarding your business. Spending
caters to my own personal interests; investing
caters to the interests of my company. So, after
weighing the risks, I invest any amounts of money
unquestioningly if they have to do with getting
more business. I also very often pay more than
the going rate for services and material if I am
getting favored treatment from my suppliers. I
never whipsaw suppliers nor pit one against the
other for mere pennies or even dollars. Relationships in these areas are more important to me.

These are hardly the sentiments of a Scrooge. No, I'm merely pointing out that your personal standard of living should have nothing to do with the health of your business (friend).

Similarly, if you are an executive in a firm, what you consider to be a living wage for you has nothing to do with the earning capacity of the company. You are only worth a higher salary than the one you are earning if your company can afford it. Most people don't seem to understand this.

Let's stop talking about spending money now and deal, instead, with the other side of the ledger - - - receivables. I often wonder if many people are aware of the enormous amounts of money which slip through the cracks of our business world. I'll give you a clue. I bought a new car for my small firm two years ago and paid for it with money accrued by dint of the fact that other businessmen forgot to invoice me for goods and services over an eighteen-month period. Conversely, I was once appointed executive director of a badly slipping chain of stores; I saved the company over $10,000 annually in the first week by merely examining each invoice before payment. The chain had been so badly managed before, that no one had done that, and various suppliers had been taking advantage of that fact. When was the last time you examined every invoice for one solid week? And when was the last time you went

through your receivables to make sure that every
penny your company has earned is paid? How strong
are your dunning methods? How meticulous are your
credit investigations?

A great number of people in business today
regard their firms as they do their homes in these
ridiculous inflationary times. By that I mean that
a home which has always been considered as perma-
nent, as sanctuary, and as our own very personal
habitat has all of a sudden become a commodity to
be sold for an enormous profit. Never mind that
it would cost as much or more to find a new home.
Similarly, people are regarding their businesses
as commodities to be sold on the open market to
any acquisitive conglomerate that comes along.
Never mind that you poured all of your creative
talents to build it; never mind that the business
will perish under the new impersonal management
(it usually does, so you can't use the stupid
rationale that you did it for the sake of the
business); never mind that you will be looking a-
round in very short order for another business to
get into (this is common); *that's no way to treat a
friend that's supported you and been so good to you all those
years.* This isn't bathos. There are too many
people *starting* businesses today with the idea of
selling it at a huge profit a few years down the
line; having started with the wrong attitude in
the first place, they wonder why their businesses
aren't thriving. If you are building your business

to sell it, you are building nothing. Oh, doing
it for the money, are you? And what does a sea-
captain do with a pocket full of money after he
has sold his ship?

Under the normal arrangement of selling a
business to a larger company, the principal usually stays on with a long-term contract as president. Indeed, the parent company prefers buying
the old management this way. But I have never
met a former owner who was completely happy with
this set-up. His complaint is that he has exchanged one set of pressures for another. Everything is fine and the romance continues until the
day that the bottom-line goes slightly awry. Then
the comptrollers from the parent company swarm in
like hornets, demanding explanations and making
accusations. At that point, the contract is usually broken - - - or the former owner is.

What is the very best way to protect this
friend we call your business? Recall that the
first definition of excellence in business in
Chapter 4 was "The ability to look ahead with
confidence in the fact that your business will
not go under." It seems to me that there are
two parallel paths we must take to gain this
confidence. First, we must be certain that we
always have enough cash reserves on hand to with-
stand any reasonably long slump or recession.
Second, we must remember that with business, as

with everything else, *small is beautiful*. You can't go home and announce that you fired every last employee, but you can keep the biggest item of expense, your payroll, down to a minimum by using temporary employment agencies, outside services and piece-work arrangements wherever possible. This is the insurance policy you should be considering, rather than some of that hokey stuff a lot of the underwriting agencies are trying to sell us.

XVII. Sticking Up For Our Side

XVII. Sticking Up For Our Side

It is most amazing that in a country which was
built upon the basic tenets of capitalism the
business community is so consistently disparaged.
Look anywhere. On TV the businessman is usually
the bad guy. If it is a murder mystery, some
wealthy businessman is most often the culprit with
greed as his motive. The big entrepreneur is also
generally portrayed as the bigot, the adulterer
or the international gangster. So much for entertainment.

Society paints us as the lethal exploiters
of consumers. For the almighty buck, we would
willingly and deliberately do anything from cre-
mating little children in flammable pajamas to
impoverishing the entire adult population. We
are out to defoliate the land and, if that doesn't
work, blow it up.

In the past thirty years there have been
literally thousands of books on the subject of
our nefarious undertakings. And how have we answered this constant barrage of insidious charges?
Practically not at all. For all of its combined
awesome power, the business community has been
particularly meek in this regard. For all the
arrogance, bluster and vocality of the average
individual businessman, the business *world* has
been virtually silent. As each new book by Ralph
Nader's "Raiders" rolls off the press with ofttimes
outrageous charges, there seems to be no book to
answer it. As each day brings hundreds of antag-
onistic editorials, there is hardly a murmur of
refutation. Could it be that we are smug? Or
could it be that we are stupid enough to think
that society is not being affected by these dia-
tribes? Could it be that we are asleep? Or could
it be that we are *lazy?*

Let's start with book publishing, since that
is the primary area of my personal expertise. Although slanted, most of these propagandistic vol-
umes are well written and well researched. (Pro-
paganda is merely what the other guy thinks.)
These books are accepted by the publishing industry
because they are appealingly written, even though
they are often sponsored in some way by "public
interest" groups of various sorts. In the past
several decades we have "countered" with corpor-
ation-sponsored books which are slipshod, abysmally

uninteresting and poorly written; moreover, they
have dealt with subjects of the narrowest interest
and are blatantly self-serving. Often they sink
to being poorly disguised advertisements for a
particular corporation or part of a public relations
campaign for a specific industry.

There are two - - - no, three, six, seven - - -
sides to every issue. Where was the book from Detroit
that attempted to answer *Unsafe At Any Speed* or *What To
Do With Your Bad Car?* (When you come to think of it,
the average automobile is an amazingly durable
and safe piece of machinery.) Books today seem to
tell the consumer/citizen what's *wrong* with everything. What's *right* about nuclear energy, the SST,
the railroads, the construction industry? Where
are all the books to tell us? Recently, for example, I was surprised to learn that there is much
to be said for clearcutting certain forests *from an
ecological point of view.* Why didn't the roadbuilders
answer Helen Leavitt's fine book *Super Highway Super
Hoax?* Why are business and industry merely cringing
under these literary attacks without retaliating in
kind?

Newspapers and government "help" by trans-
mitting their own ignorance of business to the general reader. The result is that the world out there
thinks we are a bunch of idiotic stumble-bums.
Charles Seib is ombudsman for *The Washington Post.*
Once a week he writes a column telling us what's

wrong with the news business in general and with
the *Post* in particular (a commendable exercise).
Here is his article of March 16, 1979:

A LAYMAN'S LAMENT ON ECONOMIC OVERKILL

Pass me the Valium please. I have overdosed
on economic news and I need something to bring me
down.

My problem is not that my newspapers don't
tell me enough. They shower me, flood me. But
they don't help me to put it together, to relate
the parts to the whole, if there is one. And sometimes they talk in a language I have trouble understanding.

Let me tell you some of the things I have
learned in the past few weeks and you will see
what I mean.

We'll start with oil. I learned that air-
lines are canceling flights because of fuel shortages and that gasoline stations might close on
Sundays because the oil companies are cutting
deliveries. But I also learned that the oil
companies are trying not only to maintain their
normal reserves but to increase them.

I learned that a few oil men were indicted
in an alleged $3.8 million conspiracy to sell
$5.55-a-barrel "old oil" as $10-a-barrel "new
oil." But I also learned that such finagling
may amount to as much as $2 billion, which means
that the indictments aren't even a respectable
tip of the iceberg.

I learned that the United States has agreed
to reduce oil consumption by a million barrels
a day as part of a world-wide cutback. How?
The president will tell us some day soon. Mean-
while, I learned, the government is trying - - -
apparently unsuccessfully - - - to convince oil
companies they shouldn't pay more than $18 per
barrel of foreign oil, although it kind of likes
the idea of gasoline prices getting so high we
can't afford to buy as much.

Now let's tackle the economy as a whole.

On March 2, I learned that economic indicators declined sharply in January, bolstering the theory that the economy was beginning to slow down.

Two days later, worse news: "Economy Takes Ominous Turn," read the headline in The Washington Post, "Recession Now Seems Certain."

Ominous turn indeed. The story reported that not only were we due for a "serious slump" but that it would be accompanied by "a near double-digit inflation rate" as well. So apparently inflation and recession are not unattractive alternatives but even more attractive inseparable twins. But just about that time, I also learned that an economist for the National Association of Manufacturers sees a recession as the only cure for inflation. Not twins at all, in his book.

A few days later came word that (a) wholesale prices had risen sharply, intensifying inflationary pressures, and that (b) a report would soon show corporate profits to be booming, perhaps rising at an annual rate of as much as 35 percent.

The story on the profits said the increase "may be good for the economy" but hard on the administration's efforts to hold down prices. A Wall Street Journal headline that day put it more bluntly: "Out of Control? Federal Economic Plan Turns Into A Shambles, Many Observers Say."

The federal budget? I learned that it either should be balanced or it shouldn't, depending on which hearings were being reported and who was testifying. Anyway, the real issue was not whether it should be balanced but whether the government should be forced to balance it.

The farm problem? I learned in detail how the farmers and their tractors tore up Washington's mall, but I'm a little weak on the justice of their demand for 90 percent of parity - - - and on what 90 percent of parity means.

And then there is Wall Street, the market-

place of American capitalism. I learned that
the stock market either reacts to good or bad
news or doesn't react because it saw the good
or bad news coming and reacted earlier. I also
learned that it is infatuated with companies
with names like Caesars World and Golden Nugget
and what they are going to do to the gamblers
in Atlantic City.

I could tell you all I know about interest
rates, too, but I won't. As I said, part of
my problem is with the special language of the
financial pages. It is at least as esoteric as
the jargon of sports. A case in point:

A few weeks ago, the top financial story
in The Washington Post, the paper I am paid to
read, carried this headline: "Output At A Vir-
tual Halt; Slowdown Seen As Breather." The first
paragraph of the story declared that the nation's
industrial output "slowed almost to a halt last
month," according to the government, "but ana-
lysts said the slackening was only a breather
after months of robust increases, and did not
portend a slowdown."

In ordinary English, that and similar state-
ments through the story would have meant that
we were in a real mess; the machinery was break-
ing down. But, it turned out, what it meant in
financial-page language was that the *increase*
in industrial production had almost come to a
halt. Industrial output was, in fact, at the
highest level in history.

When I said that I thought readers might
be confused by this, I was assured by the
editor responsible that it was merely financial-page "shorthand." Only the "terribly
literal minded" (meaning guess-who) would have
trouble with it. When you are reporting specialized news day in and day out, he said, you
can't load down every story with qualifiers
and explanations.

Well, maybe so. But I, for one, need all
the help I can get. And if I am ever to make
any sense out of all this stuff, they are going
to have to start working in more qualifiers and

explanations and using language I can understand.

We generally *do* know what we are doing. Allowing the media or the government to be our spokesmen convinces society that we don't. Important people are saying important things about our activities that affect us adversely - - - and no one answers. Inane utterances from high places about business go unchallenged. The President made this public announcement: "As a former businessman I am not opposed to excessive profits - - - as long as they are not derived from increased prices." What did he say? *What did that man say??* Who questioned him? No one. Who made him explain? No one. How desensitized can we get? Charles Seib is wrong in only one respect. We don't need Valium to calm us down. We need a stimulant to wake us up.

XVIII. "Burn and rave at close of day"

XVIII. "Burn and rave at close of day"

Dylan Thomas

Years ago, I had many uncles. Vignettes of the
demise of three of them linger in my memory.

One had been a leading manufacturer of men's
neckties. He enjoyed this position for almost
forty years and was respected by his trade and
by his competitors. He loved to "replay" his
big sales to Woolworth, W.T. Grant, McCrory's
J.C. Penney and others. When he was seventy
and still in good health, his wife convinced him
to sell the business so that they could move a-
way from Manhattan into a safer neighborhood.
Unfortunately, he complied. Suddenly he found
himself with nothing to do and no one to talk to.
He tried to pay social calls on his old customers,
but they were too busy doing business and had
nothing to discuss with him now that he was "no
longer in the line." In desperation, he started

to drop in on tie manufacturers just to "talk shop"
and get infusions of nostalgia; after a while, he
was regarded as an old crank and a nuisance, so
he ceased this activity. Within one year his health
failed him - - - and within two years he died.

Another uncle was a retired attorney. This
marvelous individual had reached the age of eighty-
seven by being industrious. He wrote legal trea-
tises and books (which nobody published) and applied
for and received patents for a number of innovative
gadgets (which nobody manufactured). He was always
cheerful and contentedly busy. One day, he seemed
dejected, so I asked what was troubling him. He
told me that he had just completed the final chapter of his latest book and he had just received the
documents from Washington for his latest invention
- - - and that he neither had plans nor ideas for
any further writing or experimentation. Three days
later, I visited him in the afternoon when it was
customary for him to nap; he was, as always, re-
clining on the living-room sofa, fully dressed - - -
but this time he was dead.

The third uncle had, for many years, been a
millinery manufacturer in a very small way. Some
time after he retired, his wife (my aunt) died.
Ten years later, he could no longer take care of
himself and was consigned to a nursing home. He
was eighty-three. When I visited him, he had no
idea where he was or who I was. In fact, he was

totally unaware of the world around him. His
memory was ninety-five percent gone. But his
face glowed and his voice got strong when he spoke
of what he *did* remember: the trimmings, the prices,
the purchases, the labor, the competition and the
styles of ladies' hats from 1920 to 1955.

These stories and hundreds of thousands more
like them are trying to tell us something. If you
have succeeded as a businessman by really trying,
if you have attained the status of a true professional in your field, and if your vocation and
your avocation have fused into one, then you have
nothing to retire *to* except total oblivion.

Why sell your business when you are older?
That's the one time of life when you don't *need*
that kind of money, since you have no more respon-
sibilities. That's when you can enjoy your business or your profession the most. The greatest
thing about being your own boss in the first place
is that no employer can treat you like some out-
dated Willy Loman. Why give it up now when you
need it most?

Through years of hard work, you have made
that world connection. Keep yourself plugged in
- - - forever. Keep your contacts. In the business and professional worlds age is no barrier
to constantly widening your circle of people as
long as you are competent, knowledgeable, active

and productive, i.e. *successful*. So stay successful.
Why give it up now, just when you are rounding
third base and heading for home plate?

Sure, you can *afford* to retire now. Besides
social security, you probably have a small pension
fund and a little bit of cash. That's more than
enough to get along on, considering Medicare.
"Don't I deserve a rest, after all these years?"
you ask. A rest from what? From the striving
which has kept you creative? From the anxieties
which have mothered your inventions? Do you want
to retire to total inertia like the animals in the
zoo?

Or, suppose you have been an able executive
all your life and never owned your own business.
Suppose you are approaching *mandatory* retirement.
Medical people are being tried for murder all over
the country for accidentally or deliberately pull-
ing the plugs of life-support systems for people
near death. Will you quietly allow your employer
to pull the plug of your life-support system - - -
your work? Or will you "burn and rave?" If all
else fails, you can always start a small business
of your own. After all, look at all the experiences
and contacts you have.

The ultimate message still rings true and
clear: IF YOU'RE GOING TO STRIKE OUT, YOU MIGHT
AS WELL STRIKE OUT SWINGING.

Afterword

Afterword

Afterword

Reading back over this manuscript, I find that
many of the things I have written are quite outrageous and insane, albeit true. And I am somewhat shocked that this polemic sprang from my
typewriter. I never realized that I felt so
strongly about so many things. I'm certain that
I would not have vigorously defended these principles had I been merely engaged in polite dis-
cussions about them with my friends. Writing
sometimes crystallizes one's philosophy that way.

I recall my days in the Army when any soldier
started to bitch and the rest of us jeered, "Atta-
way, soldier, tell 'em your rights." Of course,
we had no rights; and we had no freedoms. But
this country is still far ahead of any other in
the many freedoms that we citizens do enjoy. It's
just that when government starts to get oppressive,

we tend to forget them. Nothing could have been
further from the minds of our founding fathers
than the society we now live in. We shouldn't
allow this cretinous march into social oblivion.
They can't do this to us if we don't let them.
They really can't.

                              Hubert Bermont

About The Author

Hubert Bermont was born, reared and educated in New York City. He is a graduate of New York University. He spent the first ten years of his working life in the furniture industry. During that time, he served in virtually every facet: department-store merchandiser, manufacturer's representative, decorator-showroom manager and private entrepreneur. For the next ten years, he was executive director of a large chain of bookstores in Washington, D.C. During the past twelve years, he has been a book industry consultant and director of his own small publishing firm. The following is a partial listing of his clients:

Acropolis Books, Ltd.
A.F. of L. - C.I.O.
Air Force Association

American Association of Retired Persons
American Association of University Women
American Booksellers Association
American Federation of Teachers
American Film Institute
American Forest Institute
Ballantine Books
BFS Psychological Associates
B'nai B'rith
Books for Business
R.R. Bowker Company
The Brookings Institution
Catholic University
Chamber of Commerce of the U.S.
Data Solutions
Electronic Industries Association
Evelyn Wood Reading Dynamics
The Evening Star
Federation of American Societies
    for Experimental Biology
FIND/SVP
Garfinckels
Goodway
Grosset & Dunlap
Harper & Row
Human Events
Information Clearing House
International Reading Association
Journal of the Armed Forces
Kephart Communications
McGrath Publishing Company

McGraw-Hill

Metromedia

National Academy of Sciences

National Education Association

National Portrait Gallery

National Recreation & Park Association

National Retired Teacher's Association

National Wildlife Federation

Nation's Business

Optimum Book Marketing Company

Pitman Publishing Company

Performance Dynamics

Random House

The New Republic

Retired Officers Association

The Smithsonian Institution

Stein & Day

U.S. Department of the Interior

The Viking Press

WETA-TV

James T. White & Company

Index